Samuel Leeds Success Students (Volume 3)

Thirty more Samuel Leeds students share their extraordinary stories of how they have broken through the sound barrier as property investors!

Introduction

In Samuel Leeds Success Stories (Volume 3), thirty more people discuss the triumphs they have had as property entrepreneurs. The book is laden with advice as they pick out their top tips to help budding investors propel themselves to a better life.

They document their winning strategies in detail and talk openly about the profits they have made. As well as sharing the secrets of their success, some point out the mistakes they made along the way which could help others avoid the same pitfalls.

While the individuals featured come from different walks of life, cultures and age groups, they have three major things in common. They are PASSIONATE about property. They have become FINANCIALLY FREE through property, and they have gained a great amount of KNOWLEDGE from their interactions with Samuel Leeds.

The case studies in this volume are remarkable for a variety of reasons. The first chapter on Amelia Asante sets the bar high for the rest of the book. It is not every day your boss helps you to become financially independent in your early 20s – but that is exactly what Samuel Leeds did for Amelia.

The Property Investors founder agreed to take on a *Financial Freedom Challenge* with his talent manager and videographer. With his guidance, she was able to buy her own house in Manchester and live rent-free in London in the space of five days. At the same time, her bills are now covered through her earnings from property.

Two of the chapters feature students who have earned a formidable reputation for 'strong' performances in and outside their business worlds.

Personal trainer Dan Bowie lifted the WBC British Thai Boxing title in 2013. He is now 'smashing it' in the industry too, with his partner Hollie, after joining the Property Investors Academy. The former postman is making a clean profit of £12,000 a month from renting out properties he does not even own to the rich and famous.

His portfolio of three rent-to-rents includes a £1.6m town house with views of Windsor Castle. At the time Dan was interviewed he was set to complete on another one. He has also refinanced his house to buy two properties in the north of England which are being converted into HMOs.

World class strongman Ollie Clarke and his childhood friend Jamie Mcdonald had only been in Samuel Leeds' academy for a few months before they were making around £15,000 a month as deal sourcers.

Shortly after leaving school another top sportsman, 18-year-old Tom Grierson, was earning more than some of his old teachers. Tom, a semi-pro rugby player, has implemented every creative method of making money in the housing market, bar developing – and that is now in his sights.

Aydin Guner, from Liverpool, made regional and national headlines when he started lockdown with £500 in the bank and ended it as a property millionaire. In just 18 months, Aydin went from having a home with a mortgage and a steady job to becoming a serial investor in real estate, using the buy, refurbish, refinance strategy.

These are just some of the extraordinary stories featured in Volume 3. Others include a former chef who is now making tasty profits from rent-to-rents, an electrician who went on to become a bright spark in property, a musician on song with rent-to-rents, and an ex-army man marching to success as an entrepreneur.

Every student featured is an example of what can be possible in life if you get the right knowledge and are prepared to put in the work.

What is abundantly clear from all these success students is that the right attitude is as important as the right education. Take Osita Eze. He literally threw away his television to concentrate on his property journey.

His dedication paid off in style and he now has a portfolio of five rent-to-rent serviced accommodation apartments making an average profit of £3,000 a month. He has also picked up the keys to his first investment house, having previously rejected the idea of owning real estate.

Family man Kamil Domski showed that resilience is as important as dedication on his way to success. He lost count of how many rejections he had but says it felt like a least 100 'no's' before he finally got a 'yes' on a property. A year later, Kamil had four rent-to-rents in Coventry which are set to earn him as much, if not more, than he was making in his old job – for working a fraction of the hours.

Regev Farkash' story is jaw-dropping. He arrived in the UK with his dog and a £100,000 debt but is now earning thousands of pounds a month from a multi-million property portfolio.

Powerful partnerships also feature strongly in this volume, with some showing the benefits of 'keeping it in the family.' A mother and son team became financially free less than two years into their new venture, while two cousins are making £4,000 a month from properties they do not own. Two brothers also made £109,000 from a single piece of business.

ABOUT SAMUEL LEEDS

Samuel Leeds is a self-made multi-millionaire entrepreneur and the founder of Property Investors, the largest training establishment of its kind in the UK.

Still only 31, the father-of-three has completed hundreds of lucrative property deals. At the time of publication, he was working on plans to transform the Eagle Works, a former Victorian factory in the heart of Wolverhampton, into luxury apartments.

Samuel lives in a £3m property in leafy Beaconsfield and is the owner of Ribbesford House, a Grade II listed country mansion in Worcestershire which was once used by General de Gaulle to train Free French cadets in readiness for the D-Day landings during WWII.

As a committed Christian, Samuel believes that the pursuit of wealth is a force for good, especially when used to benefit others. A keen philanthropist, he is well known for his charity work with the Samuel Leeds Foundation, financing fresh water projects in remote African villages and helping to rebuild schools in the poorest areas of Uganda. He also contributes to many other worthy causes closer to home. Samuel sums himself up as a 'compassionate capitalist.'

Amazingly, as a schoolboy Samuel sat on the special needs desk on occasions. Suffering with ADHD and dyslexia, his ambitions were far from lofty when he left school at 16. He thought his destiny in life was to become a full-time binman.

However, despite having no means, Samuel bought his first buy-to-let at below market value shortly before his 18th birthday. He was too young to apply for a mortgage but got permission to put the house in his stepfather's name. After refinancing the terraced house up to its true value, he paid off the bridging loan, pocketing a monthly profit of £950 in rent.

That modest home in Bournville, Birmingham, ignited a multi-million pound business. By the time Samuel was 19, his passive income from rents dwarfed the average person's salary. He realised early in life that property investing can be the key to financial independence.

His investment strategies rely solely on knowledge and formulas, not feelings or luck. Every property in his portfolio was secured through applying the methodical strategies he now teaches his students. In recent times he has moved onto bigger commercial developments, often in the form of joint ventures.

Samuel has always maintained that the best investment he ever made was in himself. Even as a 17-year-old he had an unquenchable thirst for knowledge. Wearing an ill-fitting £30 suit from Asda, he attended specialist property networking events, constantly rubbing shoulders with successful business people.

After 'retiring' in his early twenties, Samuel quickly became bored. He then made it his mission to help as many people as possible become financially free through property, and set up a training school.

All the students featured in this book have appeared on Property Investors' *Winners on a Wednesday* YouTube series which highlights a different success story every week.

Contents

Introduction: *i*

About Samuel Leeds   *v*

Chapter 1: *Samuel Leeds makes his employee financially free!*   1

Chapter 2: *Champion Thai boxer is smashing it with rent-to-rents*   9

Chapter 3: *Teachers who became 'property pupils'
change their lives for the better*   17

Chapter 4: *Man who arrived in the UK with his dog and a
£100K debt is now making £6K a month from property*   25

Chapter 5: *Electrician proves to be a bright spark as a
full-time property investor*   33

Chapter 6: *Couple with £20m portfolio keep on learning
with Samuel Leeds*   41

Chapter 7: *Former chef makes tasty profits from
rent-to-rents after losing £19,000 on Bitcoin*   49

Chapter 8: *Property Investors helps teenager to earn
more than some of his old teachers through rent-to-rents*   57

Chapter 9: *Investor threw away TV to 'channel' all his
energy into property*   65

Chapter 10: *'Failure not an option' for investor who gave
up a top job to build rent-to-rent portfolio*   73

Chapter 11: *100 'no's' could not stop investor becoming
financially free*   81

Chapter 12 *Engineer clocks up £80K from his first deal* *after joining Property Investors Academy* 89

Chapter 13: *Property millionaire who joined academy doubles his income* 97

Chapter 14: *Academy student earns £30,000 in two months from selling deals* 105

Chapter 15: *Property millionaire started lockdown with just £500 in the bank* 113

Chapter 16: *Ex Army man marches to success with two free houses and land in the Caribbean* 121

Chapter 17: *Musician is on song with rent-to-rents and making £12k profit per month* 129

Chapter 18: *Academy student builds £2m portfolio in two years with business partner* 135

Chapter 19: *Rent-to-serviced accommodation model enhances couple's life and bank balance* 143

Chapter 20: *Property millionaire with a powerful 'why' joins academy to up his profits* 151

Chapter 21: *World class strongman shows his strengths as a deal sourcer in link-up with childhood pal* 159

Chapter 22: *Brothers make £109,000 in one deal after training with Samuel Leeds* 167

Chapter 23: *Brothers-in-law now serving hungry investors instead of café customers* 175

Chapter 24: *Rugby fan's decision to swap cup final for the crash course pays off in style* 183

Chapter 25: *Childhood sweethearts aged just 21 tie up lucrative holiday property business in Bournemouth* 191

Chapter 26: *Former hospital porter's life is transformed
by property success*   199

Chapter 27: *– Mother and son team become financially free
in under two years*   207

Chapter 28: *Two academy students make £14K in a week
from deal sourcing!*   215

Chapter 29: *From surviving on £1 frozen meals to
making a hot £10K a month*   223

Chapter 30: *– Cousins inspired by Samuel Leeds' videos
make £4K a month from rent-to-rents*   231

Final Thoughts: *–*   239

Chapter 1 – Amelia Asante

Samuel Leeds makes his employee financially free!

Samuel Leeds has booked himself into hotels in Britain and abroad, with no access to his funds, to prove that it is possible to make enough money from property in a week – not only to survive but to never have to work again.

For his first Financial Freedom Challenge, the multi-millionaire Property Investors founder changed his name and wore a disguise so that estate agents would not recognise him when he set up deals. By day seven, he was able to pay for his stay and had a recurring income from renting out accommodation which would cover all his bills – and some more.

Since then, Samuel has successfully completed similar challenges in London, Manchester, Northern Ireland and even New York where he had to grapple with different rules and a market which was alien to him.

It is not surprising, therefore, that the entrepreneur gets bombarded with messages all the time by people wanting him to help them become financially free in a week. It is a source of frustration for him, he admits.

"Sometimes people message me saying can they have a coffee with me, can you move to my house? I'm like, you've not even come to my free training because you can't be bothered to have a one-hour commute, but you want me to come to your house. Come on, let's get real."

Even when his own talent manager and videographer, Amelia Asante, asked him if he would undertake a Financial Freedom Challenge with her, he initially dismissed the suggestion.

Amelia recalls that she had just filmed a challenge with Lawton Hopwood, one of the joint winners of The Eviction competition run by Property Investors, when she 'popped' the question.

"Lawton made £11,000 from deals in the week, and he also got a piece of land. I remember sitting there thinking, I'm in a better position than he is because he'd recently been made redundant during the pandemic. I thought if he can do it, what potential could I create for myself?"

Samuel laughed off Amelia's idea, advising her to join the Property Investors Academy and then they would 'have a conversation.'

So, Amelia, then aged 24, followed his advice, recognising that she had badgered him enough previously with property-related questions, and it was time to pay for some training. A few months later – after finally persuading her employer to spend a week with her finding property deals – her average monthly profit covered all her expenses, technically making her wealthy enough to retire.

After five days, with her employer's expert help, she was able to buy her own house in Manchester and live rent-free in a plush apartment block in London alongside celebrities and affluent bankers. To top it all, her bills are now paid through her earnings from rents.

Despite this, she has chosen to stay with Property Investors because she enjoys working in a company which, in her words, is growing all the time and performing well.

Part of her remit is to invite guests onto Winners on a Wednesday, Samuel's weekly YouTube series in which he interviews some of his success students. So, it was a strange feeling, she says, when she found herself on the other side of the camera talking about how she became financially independent.

Amelia also edited a documentary about her experience, entitled Financial Freedom Movie, which has received more than 165,000 views to date.

"Until the documentary came out, I hadn't really thought about being financially free because there was so much to do afterwards. It was weird watching myself back. When everyone was messaging me well done it set in.

"It does feel incredible to know that you've got that because the one thing everyone has learnt through corona is you need more than once source of income."

Amelia joined Property Investors as a videographer after she left university with a digital media degree. And she still records the triumphs of the many people who go on to become full-time property entrepreneurs after training with the company.

It was at one such event after Amelia had finished filming and was packing away her equipment that her boss surprised her by inviting her to join him on stage.

"I remember it was at The Eviction when we were revealing the overall winner. I thought Samuel was going to say thank you for helping. Then he announced he was going to do a Financial Freedom Challenge with me. I was taken aback because I knew how busy he was after lockdown.

"I felt grateful and excited, but I realised it was crunch time, so I was a bit anxious too."

Amelia first became interested in property through her mother who had already been investing in bricks and mortar but had never had any training. After coming across Samuel Leeds online, Amelia enrolled the two of them on a Property Investors Crash Course in November 2018.

They 'absolutely' loved it, so much so that her mum Rae used her credit card to pay for some advanced training on the Deal Finding Extravaganza course. The condition was that her daughter should pay her back by securing a property deal.

"She wanted me to go instead of her because she said I would remember the information and I could relay it back to her," Amelia explains.

By now Amelia was in her third year at university and had no time to go looking for deals. But then she spotted a competition to write a description for Samuel's video on his Financial Freedom Challenge in Sheffield.

The prize was some free training with Property Investors. Amelia could not believe her luck and went on to win the competition, enabling her to repay the loan and attend the DFE.

Despite only being 21 at the time, she was confident she could make a living through property.

"I've always had a bit of an entrepreneurial spirit. In my head I thought I might set up a business after university and then put the money I made from that into property.

"Then, when I went to the crash course, I thought, why don't I go straight into property?"

Instead, fate steered her into a job with Samuel Leeds' expanding property training firm after she graduated with a first-class degree. An offer of work with a start-up company fell through due to lack of funding and her plan to move into a shared ownership flat also failed to materialise.

It meant she was free to take up a position as a videographer with Property Investors, having already gained valuable experience working in that role for the Leeds Digital Festival, the biggest event of its kind in the north of

England.

She left her home village and moved to Wolverhampton, where Property Investors used to have its headquarters, knowing that within three weeks the business would be relocating to central London.

In the first six months the young graduate was promoted twice but living in London was expensive and she still had that 'itch' to make money from property. She was also continually listening to students' 'amazing stories.'

"It got to the point where I thought I do really want to do this and the best way to do it was to do the training and take action."

Amelia and her mother both joined the year-long Property Investors Academy training programme. Amelia was keen to show she was serious about learning how to become a property investor and it worked.

Before starting her challenge, she completed all the online training but took no further action because she wanted to be a beginner, starting from scratch.

Describing herself as a 'regular girl from a regular background,' she took a week off and found herself doing a deal a day to reach her target.

On the first day she negotiated a rent-to-HMO agreement in Clapham, agreeing to pay the landlord £2,400 each month in return for being allowed to rent out the rooms herself at a higher rate.

The second day saw her clinch a rent-to-serviced accommodation deal in Windsor on a two-bedroom, terraced house with one bath in a prime location near the castle. She agreed a rent of £1,300 a month with the owner, who is based in Spain, as well as a lease option to buy it in five years' time. Faced with having to find the first month's rent upfront and a £3,000 option fee, Amelia went in search of a joint venture partner.

Using her contacts in the close-knit Property Investors community, she persuaded Evans Willie, the ultimate winner of The Eviction, and his partner Ellen to take on the lease option arrangement.

In exchange for an investment of £6,000, which includes legal costs and furniture, the couple will benefit from the capital appreciation if they choose to buy the house down the line. Even if the property only increases in value by 10 per cent, they stand to make £45,000. In the meantime, Amelia will retain the income from renting out the accommodation to visitors for short stays.

On day three, Amelia and Samuel travelled to Manchester to buy a property close to her mum's house which she could live in at weekends and rent out to lodgers to pay the mortgage. They quickly found a terraced house which fitted the bill.

Although it needed a facelift, she could rent out the two bedrooms upstairs and convert the living room downstairs into a bedroom for herself. The asking price was £190,000 but Samuel suggested she put in an offer of £179,000.

By the end of the day Amelia had lined up a 95 per cent mortgage. With no time to celebrate, they then hurried to London for Amelia to pitch a deal to investors on a 10-bed HMO in Huddersfield which she had negotiated earlier that day.

On the fourth day an investor paid £4,000 to reserve the deal which helped fund the deposit on the house she was purchasing.

"We got the deal I sold from deal sourcers on the academy. We went and checked it was all good. Then we found an investor and I negotiated to make that deal happen. I got paid £2,000 to be the middleman. I also sent the contracts over for the rent-to-HMO in Clapham and the rent-to-SA in Windsor, along with my details for the property I was buying.

"You have to be on it with your paperwork or you lose deals," says Amelia.

On the final day she collected the keys to the Clapham house and filled all the rooms after a fortnight, despite her initial concern that she would be unable to find tenants.

"I literally just put it on SpareRoom and did group viewings."

She lets it to young professionals and makes a profit of £750 a month. The Windsor SA also turned out to be a huge success.

"It has been full ever since I got it. The day I got the keys I got the first guest."

Between the two properties, Amelia expects to earn a minimum of £1,500 a month. However, the cherry on the cake was still to come. On Day five, she also set up a 'house hacking' arrangement on a three-bedroom, luxury penthouse apartment in London's Canary Wharf. Amelia will rent out two of the rooms and occupy the other one during the week, enabling her to live rent-free. This is quite a bonus as she has been paying £950 a month on renting a flat in London.

Her house in Manchester is still going through but she hopes to move into it in the next few months, giving her a weekend base instead of having to rely on her mum to put her up. The mortgage came in at 90 per cent in the end, so she plans to finance the additional amount required through sourcing more deals.

In spite of her achievements so far, the Property Investors manager has no intention of resting on her laurels. She has made £8,000 from another deal already and has another joint venture partner in the offing to take on more projects in future. And she is staying put in her job for the moment.

"I love entrepreneurship, but I also love career progression and I love the company. I want to stay around a bit longer if Samuel is happy."

Explanations of financial freedom differ from person to person, depending on their circumstances. Her definition is simple.

"If for whatever reason I didn't have my job I'm sorted. I only have to spend a few hours managing it every week. So, for me that's financial freedom because I'm free of the stress. I can do what I like."

Samuel is full of admiration for his employee: "It's been great working with Amelia. She really smashed it on the challenge and feels she has more choices in life now. Effectively I retired her, just for her to come back to work anyway! I'm really pleased she has. She's a great member of the team and I'm so proud of her.

"For me having a training business is a mission and it gives me a sense of fulfilment. Even though I don't have to work, lying on a beach forever isn't actually that much fun. Hopefully, Amelia will now be able to experience the idea of 'I don't have to do this,' from a position of abundance, and we'll get more out of her – but if not, that's fine."

*The Clapham house is making a profit of £950 a month. The highest monthly profit achieved so far on the Windsor SA has been £1,820. Amelia secured the terraced house in Manchester for £178,500 with a mortgage interest rate of 1.79 per cent, but ended up buying a three-bedroom house instead to live in at weekends. So, there was no need to convert the lounge into a bedroom.

AMELIA'S TIPS

"Get down to the *Property Investors Crash Course*. That's where it all started for me and the majority of the winners."

"Don't be scared to be a beginner. A lot of people don't come down because they're scared to be in a room with people in property. They think they will be the only person not doing things when most people who come to the crash course have never done any deals."

"Just take action, educate yourself and watch Samuel Leeds' YouTube channel."

Chapter 2 – Daniel Bowie

Champion Thai boxer is smashing it with rent-to-rents

It took retired champion Thai boxer Dan Bowie three months to clinch his first property deal, but he refused to give up. He told himself nothing could be as scary as stepping into a ring and risking not just injury, but humiliation at the hands of his opponent.

All he had to do was pluck up the courage to walk into an estate agency – not in itself a daunting task but a challenge for someone just starting out who might be worried about what to say.

"I used to think at least I'm not going to leave here with broken bones or a black eye, so I'd walk in. One of the reasons I used to get so nervous fighting was the fear of getting knocked out in front of everyone and looking like a wally."

It is a similar story when it comes to property, he says.

"There are a lot of people out there afraid of making a fool of themselves. No one wants to lose money, but if you get the training and you're confident in what you're doing – and you've got the right people around you – then you minimise the risks."

Dan had the advantage of being trained on the Property Investors Academy which enabled him finally to secure a rent-to-rent agreement. The former postman went on to bag two more, including a town house worth over £1m with views of the Queen's weekend retreat at Windsor Castle.

At a peak time in the summer, his portfolio was making him a clean profit of £12,000 a month. He also refinanced his house to purchase two properties in the north of England which are being converted into HMOs.

Dan, who won the WBC British Thai Boxing title in 2013, says his personality is to never give up but admits it was hard dealing with rejections from agents at the outset. Initially he decided to focus his efforts on finding a flat with two bedrooms and two bathrooms which he could rent from the owner and then let out at a profit for short stays. This was a recognised property strategy but despite this he found himself being cold-shouldered.

"I was getting knock backs for months. I was told you're wasting your time. We get people like you in every day. The landlords aren't up for it. The leaseholds don't allow it. It can deflate you."

It was at that point that his training kicked in. Dan knew he could set up a company let arrangement which would allow him to do precisely what he was being told he could not do. So, he kept going until eventually he established a relationship with an agent who appreciated his work ethic and could see he was genuine.

This connection led to him getting the break he so badly needed but first he had to motivate himself to venture out on a rainy day.

"There was one day, I'll never forget it, it was chucking it down with rain. It was a Tuesday. I keep Tuesdays free now so I can do my property investing. I was like, man I can't be bothered to go out. I've got no viewings or meetings, but then I had a proper word with myself. I went to this agent in Windsor I'd built a relationship with. I said to the lady, I know you were going to call me if anything comes up, but have you got anything?

"She goes, I've got this house... I knew straight away it was going to work because of the location. You can see the castle and the Thames. It had just undergone a full refurbishment. It couldn't not work!"

The property turned out to be a five-bedroom town house, valued at £1.6m, in Eton, on the opposite side of the river to Windsor. The 44-year-old ex-boxer says there was an element of doubt within him as to whether he was ready to take on a large property when he was still inexperienced.

However, he decided to press ahead after negotiating a discount on the rent from £4,000 to £3,350 a month. Buoyed by his success, Dan had little idea that he was about to go on a 'rollercoaster' journey.

Firstly, the local council informed him he needed an HMO licence, causing the landlady to get cold feet.

He insisted he would not be running the property as an HMO and persuaded the council to confirm in writing that a licence was not needed. Having got the landlady back on board, the council then advised him he needed planning permission. Again, because of his training with Property Investors, Dan was able to argue planning consent was not required, having had this confirmed by one of his coaches. Instead, the authority sent inspectors to look at the condition of the property.

Everything was found to be in order, except for a wall in the en suite on the fourth floor where there was a boiler and a water tank. The inspectors demanded it be fire proofed. The owner paid for the work to be done at a cost of £1,500 and Dan thought the last stumbling block had been overcome – only for him to be told he needed a guarantor because his business was new, and his earnings were insufficient to cover the high rent.

"I found a guarantor, a friend of mine, but then he wouldn't sign the paperwork because he didn't want them seeing his bank statements and knowing his finances.

"Then they wanted six month's rent up front, so we had to get a third joint venture partner to do the finances. We didn't want to lose the deal. Then, even after we paid six months' rent up front, they still wanted a guarantor, but they didn't want the proof of his earnings or bank statements, so he was our guarantor."

The landlady interviewed Dan and his business partner before agreeing to allow them to rent out her house at a profit in exchange for a guaranteed monthly rent.

"Her main concern was that her house was going to get wrecked. I think it was £130,000 she'd spent on having it all done up. Because it's Eton, cup of cocoa in bed at 10, she was worried there was going to be disturbance. But then when she met us, we explained exactly how we were going to run it. We said our cleaners were going to be in there two or three times a week and that if there was any damage our guests would pay for it. We also said we would give it back to her in the same condition, and she was relieved."

His partner Hollie handles the interior design and marketing. Dan attributes their success to her skill in this area. She furnished the property and opened an Instagram page to promote the accommodation.

Consequently, it has become a highly lucrative enterprise.

"Initially, it was a worry that we wouldn't be able to get people in and we would have to pay the landlord anyway, but then no. Even through lockdown we've never lost money. Our first guest came from that agent who got me it."

The guest stayed for five months, paying £7,000 per month.

"It was a dream start. It was worth all the hassle and it's smashing it still," says Dan. "We've just had a couple from America. They were there for nine months paying £7,000 a month. We had our cleaners go in every two weeks and they left it spotless. It's about £2,600 pure profit taking away the maintenance as well."

He adds: "The owner is just building another property right now in the same area in the back garden – two bedrooms, two bathrooms. She rang me up and said, 'Dan you can take that when it's done.'

Dan was employed by the Post Office for 21 years before being made redundant. At the time, he was still competing professionally and had a brick-built gym in his garden. As a sideline, he taught Thai boxing part-time.

After taking redundancy, he became a full-time coach and personal trainer, but realised that due to the physical nature of the job this was not something he would be able to do forever.

"I needed another income stream. I always had a passion for property. After talking to Hollie about what we wanted to do, we decided property was a good vehicle.

"I just engulfed myself into books and YouTube property videos and that's when I came across Samuel Leeds.

"I was a postman for six years and then I went into the cash handling side. I was the man with the helmet and the smoke and dye box making other people rich basically. But I was happy. It was good money but then the redundancies came, and I decided to take the plunge. It wasn't an easy decision."

Dan attended the free, two-day *Property Investors Crash Course* in February 2019 with Hollie. He describes it as a brilliant experience, although it took a while for him to 'get his head round' everyone getting up and dancing on stage.

"We were like, what's this about? But it was great. It was long days, but I learnt so much and I walked away feeling fired up: this is definitely what I want to do and where I want to go."

The course introduced him to the basics of property investing and opened his eyes to the strategies available to him, such as being able to refinance his house to obtain funds.

"I didn't realise I had all these options and that I could refinance and get access to some of the funds. I wasn't earning much as a personal trainer. I thought you needed a lot of money [to be a property entrepreneur]. So, I was excited."

He and Hollie went on to complete the *Deal Finding Extravaganza* programme and then immediately signed up for the Property Investors Academy, attending the *Launchpad* event in July of that year.

"We both learnt loads at the DFE. We went home that night, and we were doing the scripts driving home on a motorway. We were pretending we were talking to landlords."

Afterwards, Dan started doing the rounds of local agents in Watford where he lives.

"I didn't really get anywhere at first but then I joined the academy and went to the *Rent-to- Rent Revolution* and learnt more about rent-to-rents. That gave me the confidence to just go out there and secure my first deal."

His definition of the strategy and how it works is straightforward.

"I'm paying the landlords their rent every single month. We agree on a three-year term with a 12-month break clause. I pay all the bills. I've got a great maintenance and cleaning team. I've got a lot of things systemised now and I run it on short-term lets.

"I do use OTAs (online travel agencies) like Airbnb, booking.com, Trivago and brb. I run it like a hotel. The guests check themselves in with a key safe. They check out and then the cleaners come in and make it look all nice again."

His second rent-to-rent deal also involved a five-bedroom house in a prime location. The property is five minutes on foot from the centre of Windsor, with a drive long enough to park six Mini cars. The accommodation includes a large, extended, fully equipped kitchen diner with Bluetooth speakers, a living room and a master bedroom with an en suite. Dan negotiated the rent down from £3,500 to £3,000 per month for three years, while Hollie again took care of the design.

"We've had celebrities, footballers and influencers in there. I think it's what Hollie's done with the design. We have people contacting us regularly wanting to do video shoots and filming in there."

The boxer also rents out a flat and says that during July and August 2021 the three rent-to-rents in his portfolio clocked up a net income of £12,000 for each month.

Not content to rest on his laurels, Dan is now purchasing his own properties. He is about to pick up the keys to a converted barn as well to boost his earnings even more. His target market is wealthy individuals needing somewhere to stay for periods of a month to a year. A professional footballer has already booked to view the barn.

Dan also used the equity in his house to buy two derelict properties. One is a seven-bedroom property in Burnley which will be converted into a six-bed, all en suite HMO, with the basement turned into a two-bedroom flat.

The other property in Darlington is currently split into four flats. That one will become a seven-bed, luxury HMO and rented out to professionals.

Dan and his partner expect to pull out all their money, plus some more from the Burnley project, using the buy, refurbish, refinance strategy, which he learnt about on the academy. They expect to leave in about £10,000 each from their investment in the Darlington house. His share of the rent will be around £1,500 per month.

Samuel says: "Normally people make £500 to £1,000 per month per rent-to-rent property. You only need three or four of those and you can replace your income. Dan has got two or three of those and the profits from them are ridiculous.

"Part of his success has been down to luck. His first guests were waiting to move but then that got delayed during the lockdown and they were stuck there. Nevertheless, he deserves massive congratulations for what he's achieved so far."

DAN'S TIPS

"You need a decent 'why.' if you're just getting in there to make the money, you'll quit more easily."

"You've got to be able to just go for the 'no's and just stay positive."

"If you get the training and you've got the right people around you, you minimise the risks."

"I've made some great friends on the Property Investors Academy. Having people around me I can bounce off and ask questions and learn from is worth the fee in itself."

Chapter 3 – Jeremy Grigg and Ginny Lean

Teachers who became 'property pupils' change their lives for the better

Jeremy Grigg and his partner Ginny Lean gave up their teaching careers to go into property after seeing how it could enrich their lives.

They joined the Property Investors Academy in 2018 and spent the first year, learning about the different strategies for making money in the housing market. One of those strategies, sourcing deals for investors to buy, proved to be hugely lucrative and got them off to a flying start.

In the space of just over three years they sold 54 property deals, generating an income of £240,000.

The couple, from Cornwall, also have rental properties which bring in £9,000 to £10,000 a month and are making more money through the buy, refurbish, refinance method. In 2022, they opened an office in the seaside town of Cleethorpes in Lincolnshire which they adopted as their patch. It marked another milestone in their journey to becoming dominant players in the industry.

Like so many other students, it all began for them with the *Property Investors Crash Course.* After attending the event, Jeremy and Ginny signed up to the academy. That decision transformed their lives, setting them on the road to financial freedom.

It goes without saying that knowledge and skill have been vital ingredients in their success. Luck also played its part. Jeremy was in the right place at the right time when he set up his first major deal.

On a trip to view houses in Grimsby, just along the coast from Cleethorpes, he was staying at an Airbnb when a problem with the TV caused him to contact the owner. During their conversation Jeremy told him he was a property investor. This was something which he had been trained to do whenever he met someone new because it could result in a lead.

It led to the men meeting up again and having further discussions. Relating the story, Ginny says: "Jeremy phoned me and said this guy wants to sell one of his houses. Then, by the end of the weekend, it was he's now got 17 houses he wants me to sell!"

That portfolio, which they packaged and sold for a commission, notched up a profit of £65,000.

The very first deal which they made money on came about in equally unlikely circumstances. The fee on that deal was £3,500 but it fell through the next day. An investor subsequently bought it for £4,000, only for it to collapse again when the buyer went to Thailand.

"He still paid us, but that's not the most bizarre thing about that property," recalls Jeremy. "The vendor said I've had enough of investors. I'm going to put it on the market through an online agent. Ten months later he came back to me and said I still can't shift this property.

"It's a five-bedroom HMO with grandfather rights. In our area grandfather rights are worth a fortune. We ended up getting that property on a lease purchase agreement."

Jeremy and Ginny negotiated an option to buy the house for £92,000 after four years and are about to exercise their right by using investor finance. The property is now valued at £150,000, giving them an uplift of nearly £60,000, in addition to a regular income.

"It cashflows really well. The rents turnover is something like £2,000 to £3,000. It probably earns us £1,100 a month," explains Jeremy who left his teaching job in 2017.

"It was always a means to an end teaching for me," he adds. "I went to university because my mum really wanted me to go. I went into teaching because everybody else seemed to be going into teaching.

"I taught and there are elements of it I really enjoyed. It's a buzz. But teaching for me became almost suffocating. It was the system that was the suffocation. You're expected to go up the ranks and take more on."

He describes property as something burning inside him for as long as he can remember. When he went into business with Ginny, they had five flats in Cornwall which were rented out as single lets. One was acquired in 1992 and the other four in 2008. These properties were providing a basic income, but they were highly leveraged, which meant there was more debt than equity in them.

In hindsight, Jeremy says it was a classic case of a landlord who gets a few properties trying to manage his portfolio with 'no science behind it.'

All that changed when he attended a *crash course* led by Samuel Leeds who spoke about the basics of property investing and set the audience practical tasks. Jeremy was hooked straight away by what he had seen and heard and urged Ginny to return with him when the event was repeated.

"I came along not really sure what to expect. I can honestly remember being completely and utterly gobsmacked about how amazing it was," says

Ginny. "From the minute we walked in the door it was two full days of just thinking this is mind blowing.

"I was so impressed by Samuel. It was massively inspirational and educational. We met some fantastic people and started to develop a good base to increase our property knowledge from."

Afterwards they signed up for the academy and completed the *Deal Finding Extravaganza* as part of their training.

Jeremy says: "I didn't even know what a deal sourcer was until the first session we had in Birmingham. We had a massive negative net worth. We'd both come out of different marriages, and we were really struggling. We'd given up homes and we were renting. Samuel just looked at our figures and said, 'You need to be deal sourcers.'

After selling a string of deals and loving every second of it, he and Ginny are now both full-time property entrepreneurs.

Ginny realised two years into her training that she no longer needed her job and handed in her notice after 28 years in the teaching profession. Then Covid struck and her school persuaded her to come back. She stayed for another two years but has now 'finished forever.'

It gives her the freedom to spend more time with Jeremy in Cleethorpes where he is continually looking for new opportunities.

After bringing in a 'fast pound' through selling deals, they have progressed to buying and renovating dilapidated houses which they then remortgage to their new value once the work is finished. This allows them to draw out a chunk of cash to reinvest in more property ventures.

Ginny says the academy was a massive eye-opener to the possibilities in property, including the BRR strategy which they have used for most of their acquisitions.

Jeremy spotted the potential, while they were on the academy, to also make money from HMOs. They already had a property in Cornwall which was being rented out, but not on a room-by-room basis which he came to realise was more profitable than a single let. So, they refurbished it and completed the process of making it compliant as a house share.

By switching tactics that one now cashflows really nicely, says Jeremy.

That positive experience gave them the confidence to take on more.

Ginny says: "We've just got two that are now up and running in Cleethorpes that were bought with investor finance – high end HMOs, six beds, six en suites.

"When the valuer came round to one of them, he said it was one of the best he'd seen in that area for a long time. It's really impressive. That's what I've loved, seeing the end result."

The purchase price of the Victorian house was £140,000, with the refurbishment cost coming in at £83,000. The property was then refinanced on a commercial valuation of £275,000. It cemented what turned out to be an excellent investment.

"The day before the valuation the NHS trust in the local area, which is providing quality housing for overseas nurses and doctors, took on the whole property on a six-month agreement. The rent is £3,700 a month. So that just took it straight off our hands. The valuer couldn't argue with that," adds Jeremy.

Their entire portfolio cashflows £9,000 to £10,000 a month on a turnover of £15,000 and an occupancy rate of 95 per cent.

Whilst it would be easy for Jeremy and Ginny to take their foot off the pedal, they have no intention of retiring just yet. In fact, their business is expanding all the time. They have four more properties going through the conveyancing process.

One is a three-storey, ex-council office block. They have taken over the ground floor and will own it through the business. The top two floors will be converted to create four, two-bed apartments in what will be their first commercial to residential project.

"We've also got two BMV (below market value) flats going through which we picked up at a very nice price," explains Jeremy. "We know we can remortgage in 12 months' time and we'll get that money back out.

"There's also a commercial unit on the back of a four-bed HMO which is sat on the market because uneducated people just don't understand it. We've got a good broker who said we'll put that on a commercial loan, and we can refinance that further down the line."

Two relatives are investing in their property too, he points out. Another scheme being planned is to convert a garage the size of a sports hall into flats.

"We've got a planning application going through now. I want to be able to create some passive income for my mum. At this stage of life for her it would be awesome. One of my brothers was following me on social media checking what we were doing and now he's involved too."

Ginny agrees that their business is gathering momentum. "I've made this leap of faith and I really want to see how far we can go with this. That's what's so exciting because it's something so different to everything that I've done before."

With a base now in Cleethorpes, Jeremy is becoming known in the town.

"We've got our base up in our patch. That makes you part of the community. I went out for a drink one evening and people are starting to recognise me. They say, 'You're that property guy, aren't you? Oh yeah, my aunt's just getting rid of her place.

"If you put yourself out as a presence, people come to you with the deals which is fantastic."

That connection to the area is strengthened by working closely with the local council. "The housing enforcement team up there love it when people are putting back quality, compliant property. That's what we want to do and make a name for it."

Making the transition from being a teacher to becoming self-employed has been challenging at times. One of the skills Jeremy and Ginny have had to acquire is learning the art of selling.

"It didn't come naturally to me. I had to work hard at that. I've got better. I've had experience of running a network marketing business, but I think teachers find sales naturally difficult."

Ginny agrees, describing it as a 'different world.' Jeremy admits it has been a hard slog as well over the last few years and they frequently live at opposite ends of the country. However, they look forward to holidays. They also make time to return to the Property Investors Academy as mentors.

Education remains close to their hearts. This is something they have in common with their guru Samuel. The Property Investors founder has given talks in London and Leicester to schoolchildren about how they can go into business instead of assuming their only choice is to get a job or go to university. He is keen to see financial literacy put on the curriculum both in Britain and in Uganda where he has built a school.

Ginny too wants to share her knowledge with students and to show that someone like her, who had no background in property, can be successful in that field.

"I also want to show my kids that there is a very different way and hopefully then that's something that can be passed on to others."

Jeremy agrees: "What Samuel is doing is helping others get financially free.

I would love to go back and teach again, but with somebody who really wants and would benefit from what I'm teaching."

He adds: "You don't have to run a business. If you want to carry on being employed, just make your money work for you. Learn what passive income is what and an asset is."

They are both full of praise for the academy. Jeremy says that for a year it provided them with exactly what they needed and was 'formatted in the right way, at the right time.' It also gave them business associates who they still work with. They also help out from time to time as mentors.

Samuel is equally complimentary about them. He says: "Jeremy and Ginny have done amazingly well. I'm really pleased with their success but I'm also grateful for them coming back into the Property Investors community. I always say when you hit the mountain tops you've got to pull people up with you. That's exactly what they're doing."

JEREMY AND GINNY'S TIPS

"You don't have to run a business, but if you want to carry on being employed just make your money work for you. Learn what passive income is and what an asset is."

"Don't get too wrapped up in just the success of the business. Enjoy life as you go along and celebrate the successes."

Chapter 4 – Regev Farkas

Man who arrived in the UK with his dog and a £100K debt is now making £6K a month from property

Property multi-millionaire Regev Farkash jokes that he is the 'broke, rich guy' because he is constantly investing his cash in real estate. As Regev describes it, he does not want to hold back any money in his pocket as his ambition is to keep growing his business and leave a legacy for his family.

For someone who was desperately poor only a few years ago, it is quite a statement. But then Regev has come a long way since emigrating from Israel to England with his beloved Jack Russell in tow.

He arrived in this country in 2014 with just £50 to his name and a debt of £100,000 weighing him down. Refusing to let that get in his way, the father-of-one lifted himself out of poverty by becoming a property entrepreneur.

Starting out with rent-to-rents, he has built up a portfolio worth around £3m with the help of joint venture partners. His share of the equity amounts to £500,000, while the rents give him an income of £6,000 a month.

Regev may be continually recycling his capital into new projects, but it is this steady cashflow which affords him a comfortable lifestyle in London with his wife and two-year-old daughter. His monthly outgoings include £2,000 to rent a flat, kindergarten fees of £1,000, and the same amount for food. He also runs two cars and takes regular holidays.

"We have whatever we need and want, so it's not quite true to say I'm broke!" Regev admits.

The contrast with his former life, which was one of daily struggle for survival, could hardly be greater. One of the few jobs he could find when he first came over was working as a poorly paid labourer in the construction industry and it was hard work. His back ached from digging the ground with a shovel and he had holes in his shoes.

There were days when he would even go without food so that he could feed his dog Jack who lived with him in a modest room in a house share.

"It was the worst time of my life. I used to look at the mirror and not even recognise myself. I never cried in my life. That was a period that I used to cry a lot," Regev remembers.

Even so, he was grateful to be employed. It meant he could pay his rent and eat, although there was little money left after having to pay off another debt and find his bus fare.

"I used to get £70 per day and repay a small debt here in the UK to a friend who helped me pay my rent. I gave him back £30 from the £70. So basically, I made £40 every day. I borrowed £3,000 just to hold myself alive. It wasn't easy but I was very happy to work."

Despite the hardship Regev endured he remained resolute and upbeat.

"It was horrible but in my mind was: it's a period of time. It will pass. Everything will be just fine, and you need to continue [moving] forward."

Realising labouring was taking him nowhere, Regev started looking for ways to make more money. He was 35 and with a slipped disc the time was right for him to try to change his life. If ever an opportunity came his way, he used to 'grab it with both hands.'

So, when his employer bought a large house in North London which was uninhabitable, Regev jumped at the chance to boost his earnings. There were a few windows missing, the carpet was old, and it needed a fresh lick of paint. To Regev this was all 'small stuff' which could be fixed. He, therefore, offered to rent the property for 18 months and renovate it at the same time.

The two men agreed on a rental of £1,000 per month, out of which Regev deducted the £6,000 cost of doing up the house, leaving him with £500 to pay in the first year. He drafted in the owner's employees to help him with the work, and it was finished very quickly.

The deal turned out to be hugely profitable.

"I used to make £3,000 a month because the rooms in North London are expensive. I was getting £800-900 per room, and it was a big house, so it created a very nice cashflow."

It enabled him to start paying off his £100,000 debt and from there Regev moved on to taking on buy, refurbish, refinance schemes with joint venture partners. Regev now has his own construction company, along with a portfolio of five properties in London.

Key to his success, he says, was his training with Property Investors which taught him how to find deals and introduced him to the buy, refurbish, refinance, rent strategy.

He first became aware of the BRR strategy during the pandemic when he was spending more time at home.

"I was searching for what I can do with the money I have saved in property.

I googled house flips and straight away Samuel Leeds appeared with his video about BRR. I started to listen. I was like oh my god, if this is actually real, with my construction company I can make it happen."

Regev joined an online training programme run by Property Investors during the lockdown to increase his knowledge and improve his skills. He also studied Samuel's other YouTube videos.

"I know all of them by heart and I loved the training. I felt like it was feeding my soul because I knew I was in the right place. I knew I needed to gain as much knowledge as I could. It's a game of big money this for me and I wanted to reduce the risks as much as possible and get as many gold nuggets as I could."

He completed the *Deal Finding Extravaganza* programme in record time and spent a day-long mentoring session with Samuel at his home after the restrictions were lifted. When the event was advertised, Regev was the first person to book a place.

"I wasn't going to miss a good opportunity. At the time I didn't know Samuel personally. I thought, that's the time to meet."

He adds: "I think my biggest value is that I am a man of action – massive action. Even today when all my equity is invested, I'm putting offers on houses – OK, £1.3m? No problem. When I get an offer accepted, then I start to run in search of the investor."

After attending the DFE and meeting Samuel, he went looking for his first deal as a trained entrepreneur and came across a one-bedroom ground floor flat right near to his home in the north London suburb of Edgware.

"I thought I can do an extension and then it will be three bedrooms. It will be like an HMO and then what will the value be? I started to do the calculation and I realised wow it's 100m from my house. My cost prices are lower because I'm the contractor. It's all come together. OK, that's my first deal."

As a first-time buyer, he needed to raise finance. So, he sought advice from a mortgage broker who was renting one of his rooms. His broker was so impressed with the deal which Regev had found that he promptly offered to fund it, as well as a second venture.

With £75,000 of equity left in his hand, Regev decided that would be enough for half an investment in another deal and applied for a bridging loan from a local provider.

'When he saw the deal, he said: why do you need to get a bridge? I can join in with you. I replied: alright, let's go for it."

Not everything has gone Regev's way. The owner of one property pulled out after an agent advised him that he was selling his property too cheaply.

"I was very disappointed but after one month the agent called me and said the deal is back on the table, but he wants £10,000 more. I said alright, no problem. We have a deal.

"I paid £370,000, plus £10,0000 stamp duty and £60,000 for the renovation – so a total of £440,000."

The property in question was a two-bedroom flat on the first floor of a house. A third bedroom was created by extending into the loft. Some of the walls were also removed to make it open plan and ultra-modern with high specification fixtures and fittings.

The investment paid off as the flat was subsequently valued at £600,000.

This will allow him to pull out all the money invested by refinancing the property to its new value.

"It's 100 per cent out plus £160,000 equity on the property. I've done four deals like that. One of them is a whole house that I split into two. So, five properties. I renovated them at the same time and I'm in the process of refinancing them.

"I'm not leaving any money in any of the five properties. I'm getting all the money back. Those are the kind of deals I'm looking for from the beginning."

It feels good, says Regev, to no longer be poor, but he is not ready to celebrate just yet.

"It's given me some relaxation but on the other hand when you come from a place that's so low it leaves you with some mental scratches. You're always afraid to be there again, so it's hard to jump and dance and be over the top because of it. First, I want to reach my goals and then I will celebrate. I want to grow and grow until I reach my target."

With his 12-year-old Jack Russell still his faithful companion, Regev is as hungry as ever to achieve more success after leaving school at 15.

"I always had the feeling don't stay behind anyone. Run in front of everyone. This is my motivation in life, and this is what triggers my massive action. I don't want to stay behind.

"In property I love everything. It starts for me from the build. The build side is interesting and profitable. Also, from the investment side, who doesn't want to leave a legacy for his family? It's something that will stay after me."

He is grateful to his wife for supporting him throughout his journey.

"I met her when I was broke. She believed in me. She took me from the floor and I respect her for that."

And, of course, he is thankful to Samuel Leeds. He chose Samuel to train with, he says, because he had the most energy of all the property trainers around and felt a connection with him.

"We have quite a similar story. He quit school when he was young and is a believer. I think we have many points in common."

Samuel says he has been delighted to see how Regev has flourished with the help of Property Investors.

"A lot of people say hard work leads to prosperity. I believe hard work does not lead to prosperity. It's about working hard but also smart at the same time. Regev has done that. He is great at putting people together and has pulled in some amazing joint venture partners who have teamed up with him to help him get where he's got to.

"It shows the power, not just of surrounding yourself with good people and taking action, but also of finding a good deal. If you find a good deal the finance will come.

"Regev also has a really great energy about him. No one can meet him and forget him. He might not have had much money to start off with, but he had the construction knowledge and the ability to find the deals off the back of the videos and the training. So, he's bringing quite a lot to the table."

*Regev now has a £7m portfolio and is buying more properties in his area.

REGEV'S TIPS

"I came here broke because I over-leveraged myself in my own country, but it is possible to start with nothing and succeed in property."

"To anyone who wants to do what I did I would say believe in yourself."

"Take massive, massive action."

"Don't be afraid. You will gain confidence with the success of your moves. If you don't make your moves, it's not going to happen."

Chapter 5 – Thomas Atkinson

Electrician proves to be a bright spark as a full-time property investor

Electrician Thomas Atkinson had the perfect start in life. He had a trade which rewarded him well and a house which he shared with his fiancée. There was, however, a price to pay for this seemingly idyllic existence.

Thomas worked away a lot and could see that there would always be a ceiling on his earnings as an employee. So, when he realised he could make more money in property, he left his £48,000 a year job.

That was in January 2021 and it proved to be a sound decision. These days the 25-year-old entrepreneur earns an average of £5,600 a month by selling deals and making money from doing up and renting out houses. Thomas specialises in the buy, refurbish, refinance and rent strategy, acquiring rundown properties both for himself and investors. So far, he has bought four houses, ploughing the proceeds from each one into funding his next purchase.

His career in property began accidentally when he and his partner Shona were carrying out some improvements on their own home, for themselves rather than to make money. Thomas happened to watch some of Samuel

Leeds' YouTube videos and learnt that once they had finished the work the house would be worth more. He would, therefore, be able to take out a mortgage based on the new value which would give him funds to invest in real estate.

"We bought the house for £154,000, spent £15,000 on it and it revalued at £210,000 in six months. So, it was an accidental buy, refurbish, refinance [scheme]," explains Thomas.

After refinancing the mortgage, he was left with £50,000 in his pocket. He invested £12,000 of it in joining the Property Investors Academy in 2019, despite his friends and family being highly sceptical.

"I remember signing up to the academy and coming home and mum was like, what have you done?" He laughs at the memory but then adds seriously: "I said, no trust me. I want to make it work. I believe in it."

Thomas was confident he was doing the right thing because he wanted to be self-sufficient and not have an upper limit on what he could earn.

"I was in Glasgow for three months and the people I was around I could see weren't happy. They'd been doing the job I was doing for 10 years, and they had children. I could tell that they wanted to be at home with the children and there was a cap on what they could earn.

"If I wanted to get further than I was, I needed to be a director which was very unlikely. The whole drive to invest in property was so that I could be there for the children when I'm older."

Thomas got back his academy fee through the equity on his first deal. He and his fiancée bought a house in Hull for £63,000. The refurbishment, legal fees and the deposit for the bridging loan came to £40,000. Once the work was complete, the property was refinanced to its new value of £97,500.

"We left in £11,000, so we pulled most of our money out. Then we did it again. That deal was pretty much identical to the second one because we bought a house on the opposite street for £65,000.

"The refurb was a bit more on that because we had a good power team in place. The fees came to about £45,000 all in, including the bridging and deposits. We refinanced at £110,000 and left £9,000 in that. The return on investment on both was about 30 per cent."

Thomas became go adept at finding investment opportunities in the housing market that soon people were asking him to bring his deals to them. One of those people was another academy member, Patrick Welsh, who began co-deal sourcing with him.

He sold his first deal through Patrick while still working as an electrician full-time and they shared the £5,000 commission. An investor bought the property in York as a BRR project.

Thomas went on to sell five more deals as a co-deal sourcer but then hit a lean patch and sold none. It was only when he enrolled on the academy's bespoke *Accelerated Coaching and Mentoring Programme* that his fortunes changed.

Thomas came under the scrutiny of Samuel Leeds himself who looked at his performance and targets. It was a brutal two days as students on the course were divided into two groups – those who were 'winning' in property and those who were struggling.

When Samuel asked him what his problem was, Thomas explained he had not sold a deal for two months and was worried.

"Samuel looked at my diary and there wasn't much in there. I said: 'I go to the gym in the morning, and I walk my dog.' He said: 'So, you're not actually starting your day till 10 o' clock in the morning. I needed a shake basically to get my head back in gear. I think I was getting too comfortable."

Working at weekends and again reflecting on the fact his pay was always going to be restricted, Thomas concluded he would be better off going into property which he had long been interested in.

"As soon as I saw you could make a lot of money through deal sourcing, I just thought you can achieve a lot more in property. I knew how hard I worked being employed. If I put that into my own business I could do really well."

After the accelerated coaching programme, in June 2021, he had a 'reboot.'

"I had to put everything back on paper and think what I was doing wrong – what was working and not. The comments from some of the mentors pushed me in the right direction. Now I'm selling deals to investors directly and it's really worked."

Thomas also attended the *Samuel365 Mastermind* session where he was able to report to Samuel that he had made £7,000 that month and answered questions from other students.

"Before I did the *Accelerated Coaching and Mentoring Programme,* I didn't realise how much you need to concentrate on finding investors. I was concentrating on deals and not investors."
Through social media he built up a mailing list of investors to whom who he could offer his buy, refurbish, refinance deals. He also handles the project management for his clients and has found an excellent build team in Hull.

He completed the restoration for his first BRR venture himself. This stretched him as he was still a full-time employee, living in York and commuting to Hull – although the work cost him only £15,000. Now he oversees projects while his build team takes over, charging £20,000 for a standard, three-bedroom terraced house.

Thomas not only identifies a property, he also negotiates the price and does his due diligence to make sure it is a good investment.

"You've got to get your building quote right. The three figures that matter are purchase price, refurbishment cost and end value. People under-estimate the refurb and over-estimate the end value.

"If you get that wrong, suddenly it doesn't make money and you might as well just have a turnkey investment."

The young entrepreneur gets his figures right by having a detailed conversation with his builder, going through a spreadsheet to ensure every aspect of the work is taken into account.

"When I view a house, I video the inside and send it to the builder. I also go through my spreadsheet to make sure everything is ticked off and it will pump out a figure to make sure it's an exact quotation to the pound of what it's going to be. We always add on a 20 per cent contingency to make sure there's enough of a buffer."

Thomas adds: "I'd happily pay a sourcing fee for a great deal, even if I don't find it. I think a sourcing fee is nothing compared to what you can make."

Thomas' average charge is £3,000 per deal. He sold three deals to the same investor. One was a buy, refurbish, refinance deal in Darlington. Thomas picked up a £5,000 fee for that one as it included project management. The investor also bought two family lets which Thomas had sourced, making him £9,000 in total.

Thomas finally won over his family and friends, including his mother. They all now want him to find investment properties for them.

The Property Investors Academy has been hugely influential in elevating him onto the increasingly crowded rostrum of students who have become financially free through the training. Fellow academy members have helped him along the way too, particularly Patrick who advised him about co-deal sourcing.

"It's not easy and you do need good support around you to keep pushing you through those rough patches."

At the accelerated coaching programme, Thomas confided in Patrick that he was thinking of going back to his old job for two days a week because he could not sell a deal and had bills to pay. Thankfully, Patrick and another coach dissuaded him.

"I would definitely have gone back to work if it wasn't for the programme. If I was speaking it, I was going to talk it into reality. I probably would have gone back to being a full-time electrician."

The highlights on the academy for him were the *Deal Selling Masterclass* and the *Buy, Refurb, Refinance* courses which gave him the confidence to sell deals to investors.

The key to success with the BRR strategy, he says, is not to overpay for the property and to get it in a dilapidated state. Speaking to builders to get quotations and having a good spreadsheet are also important in estimating the refurbishment cost.

He calculates the end value by comparing the prices of similar properties on the same road. Sites like PropertyData and DealSource also provide an analysis service.

Thomas is involved in a joint venture with another academy member, Dan Bowie, to convert a house in Darlington into a six-bed HMO. They are about to complete the purchase of the house for £105,000. The refurbishment cost is estimated at £65,000 and the end value is expected to be £210,000. They will each leave around £10,000 in the deal, and it will cashflow about £1,200 a month which they will split between them. Thomas has also had another offer accepted on a property in Rochdale.

He pays tribute to his partner Shona for being a 'massive support' through his journey in property and handling his emails while he is out on the road looking for deals.

"We worked really hard to buy that first house and renovate it, and then to refinance it. It wasn't easy doing that."

They subsequently sold their first house and were able to move into a four-bedroom detached house on the outskirts of York a year after Thomas joined the Property Investors Academy.

Samuel is highly impressed by Thomas' progress: "He started by coming to the *Property Crash Course* and has come back again and again, as well as joining the academy. He's successfully sold to investors and has got a good reputation. In the Property Investors community everyone talks positively about him. People say they've bought a deal from him, and it's gone really well.

"Packaging a deal and selling doesn't take that long. If you just do one a month, you can replace the average salary. Thomas is living proof of that. He's also successfully combining the strategies of BRR, deal sourcing, HMOs and joint ventures."

THOMAS' TIPS

"Have the right power team around you. A good solicitor is so important."

"Believe in yourself and put the work in. Hard work always pays off."

"You can watch as many videos as you possibly can but until you start building your own network and having people around you, you won't really act on it. You need people to bounce off."

"The advantage of co-deal sourcing is you don't need to be compliant, so someone will sell the deal for you. The advantage of selling it yourself is you get double the money and you know who the investor is. I like to know what's been sold and the whole story behind it."

"My patch for the next year or so will be Darlington. It has an Amazon warehouse, and 750 Treasury workers are moving there. They are also spending £100m on the train station in the next five years, so I believe now is the time to invest there."

Chapter 6 – Lee and Jo Gough

Couple with £20m portfolio keep on learning with Samuel Leeds

Lee and Jo Gough have a portfolio of more than 150 properties worth around £20m, but that did not stop them from enrolling on one of Samuel Leeds' popular crash courses.

The couple believe it is never too late to learn something new and were so impressed they attended two more of Samuel's introductory courses. They even sent their teenage son Rocco to the event, which inspired him to raise finance for his first property acquisition.

It was because of this and the fact Lee and Jo love Samuel's YouTube videos that they agreed to share the secrets of their own success on *Winners on a Wednesday*.

Lee's story of how his property career began is a remarkable one. He was working as a hairdresser when he bought his first house at the age of 21 for £44,000. Within six months it was worth just £36,000. Many people would have thrown up their hands in horror, but Lee sensed an opportunity. His logic told him that it was a good time to buy when the prices were so low. So, he carried on saving to put down a deposit on another property.

The banks, however, disagreed. They refused to lend him the money for his second house, telling him it was a bad investment. Eventually, he turned to his own bank for help.

"I read a book which said you don't know how close you are to success if you give up. I thought I'm not going to give up, so the last place I was going to try was my existing bank who wouldn't give me an overdraft for £100," Lee recalls.

When he explained to the bank manager that he had managed to save the deposit, he looked at him and replied: "Right, we're going to give you a chance."

Lee still had to produce a profit and loss forecast but he got his loan. Slowly, he grew his portfolio, based on the principle of 'buy it, rent it out and sit on it.' By the time he met his future wife, Jo, who was also a hairdresser, he had acquired eight properties. It was only two months into their relationship that she found out about his mini property empire.

"He kept it quiet at first. I think he didn't want a girlfriend who was just after him because he had eight houses."

She discovered Lee's sideline when she was at the salon and saw him receiving large bundles of money which turned out to be from his tenants.

"I was a little bit suspicious at first. I was thinking where's all this cash coming from every day. I knew he was an honest guy, but I didn't know at the time it was the rent money. In those days tenants paid by cash.'

Then one day she asked him why he was always running somewhere during his breaks. He replied that he was dashing between estate agents to arrange property viewings.

Unbeknown to Lee, Jo, who was a single mother, was also saving hard to put down a deposit on a two-up-two-down where she could live with her daughter.

Lee remembers that on one of their early dates he went round to her place and spotted a picture of a small house on the wall.

"I looked at this picture and said: 'what's that?' She said: 'it's my dream house. I've got a five-year plan.' I said: 'It seems a long plan to get that. When I asked her how much she had saved and she said not very much, I replied, 'Let's look at some properties today.'

"I said: 'You've got a credit card. If you can't afford it, the rent will pay the interest on the credit card.

"We looked at some show homes and I bought a house that day," says Jo. "I was dreading going home and telling my parents, but it was the best thing I ever did. I still have the house to this day."

Lee sprung his own surprise on her when she returned from a week away with her family and he announced he had bought 11 flats.

"I read this book by Russ Whitney. It said that if all the figures stack up just go for the deal. I met two property investors and they had some flats for sale, one block of six and a block of five. The figures worked out and I borrowed the deposit on credit cards and bought them. I've still got those today too."

At the beginning, Lee lived way below his means to save the deposit for his next house. He admits it was an 'old-school' strategy, but the purchase of the flats and his advice to Jo reflected a change in his thinking. He realised he could use other people's money to expand his business.

Lee also became aware of creative strategies, such as rent-to-rent and lease option agreements which would offer him far more options when investing in property.

Over the years Jo has become skilled herself at making money from bricks and mortar and they are still active investors. They have properties from

Penzance to Sunderland, as well as abroad. Their portfolio is made up of a mixture of residential lettings, commercial property and holiday lets in the UK, Portugal and Spain which they manage between them, aided by their power team.

Despite their wealth of knowledge and experience, they are both eager to keep on learning which is why they signed up for a virtual *Property Investors Crash Course* during lockdown.

"Right from the beginning we've always attended everything we could possibly attend, networked wherever we could, learnt something wherever we can," explains Jo.

Lee describes the crash course as a fantastic experience and one they repeated. Covid restrictions meant the first two events, which they joined, had to take place online, but later they were able to go along to the live version and see Samuel in action.

"The enthusiasm and inspiration Samuel Leeds gives everyone is amazing, and you can always learn something. It doesn't matter how small it is. When you're out in business you think, ah there's something else I could do here. Maybe that strategy won't work but this will. I made some good contacts as well," says Lee.

He bought his first house before Property Investors' 30-year-old founder was even born and saw the value of his estate soar during the 1990s. Since then, from initially purchasing buy-to-lets, the couple's investments have embraced a range of strategies.

In 2020, they bought a commercial property in Torquay with a joint venture partner. It had a shop on the ground floor with offices above and was originally offered at auction for £200,000. They paid £125,000 for the premises after it went under the hammer three times and no one bid for it.

Lee believes would-be investors were put off because the rates on the ground floor were about £30,000 a year and there was no tenant in place, which created a liability straight away. It would also be extremely hard to obtain finance as commercial properties are valued according to their rental income and the shop was empty.

"We knew if we reduced the space on the commercial element, we could get the rates exempt," says Lee.

The building is now divided into two separate units, meaning there are no rates to pay. They also reduced the rent 'massively.'

"We can afford to now we've only paid £125,000 for it. We're getting rent in at £15,000 a year from the shop and suddenly it's all paying for itself. Then we will apply for permitted development for the upper floor to convert it into two flats. That's going to cost us around £100,000. The end value is going to be about £450,000."

The flats will be let out as serviced accommodation and should each bring in around £15,000 per annum as Torquay benefits from major regeneration in the months ahead.

He adds: "The partner is cash rich and doesn't want to get involved in dealing with tenants or builders. He's put some of the money in. We're 50-50 on it."

By joining forces with another investor, it allows the couple to spread their own pot of money for reinvesting in more projects.

Jo says: "This is a guy we've been working with for years. He gets a good return, so he's happy as well."

Lee and Jo are both self-made. They have never had any inheritances and nor do they intend to fund their son on his way up the ladder. Instead, they have taught Rocco everything they know about property and helped him secure his first deal. They also made sure he went to the *Property Investors Crash Course.*

Over the years their son has absorbed a lot of information about property investing but hearing it from someone else made all the difference, says Lee.

"Our experience has been invaluable too. He's learning so much about EPCs (Energy Performance Certificates) and the tenancies."

Now aged 17, Rocco was 16 when he found a property in Durham which looked like a good investment. He obtained it for £36,000 at auction after working out the figures with his father's assistance and finding an investor who is getting a fixed return of five per cent.

Rocco also set up his own limited company to run the property which he is renting out for £450 a month.

His parents are proud of his achievement and his enthusiasm to carry on learning. During lockdown his father spent an hour every day training him via Facetime from Portugal, while Jo was in England with their two children.

The whole family is now back in England after living in Portugal for six years and moving into a Georgian manor house in Devon. They bought the property because it came with cottages on the land which they could rent out. Without that income potential they would not have acquired it, says Lee.

Commercial considerations have influenced where they live before. Lee negotiated one lease option agreement which proved to be highly profitable.

He met a developer who was struggling to sell his property because it had no kitchen or bathroom which made it unmortgageable. Lee agreed to pay the owner around £800 a month with an option to buy it over the next two years for £225,000.

After moving in, he installed a kitchen and a bathroom and made other improvements costing £150,000. A few years later, after exercising his right to buy, Lee sold it for £575,000.

"It was our principal residence, so we didn't pay any capital gains tax. It gave us a clean profit of £200,000."

They pulled off another extremely lucrative deal in 2020 when they purchased a pub and a cottage which were being sold together. They paid £80,000 for the pub and £141,000 for the cottage and then spent about £5,000 on refurbishing the house.

"It was on Rightmove but with a commercial agent. The cottage should have been with a residential agent, so they were selling it on a commercial basis. It was way undervalued. We've Just had it valued at £350,000 and now we're applying for planning permission to turn the pub into two flats. There's so much money to be made from property."

Lee makes the point that if he found himself without a penny to his name, but still had all his knowledge of property, he would not start saving again to invest in houses.

"That takes too long and it's very painful. If I was starting again, I'd do rent-to-rents or other strategies you can do with little or no money, like deal selling. We've sold three deals which we didn't want to do ourselves at the time either because we didn't have funds, or they matched someone else's criteria."

Samuel agrees: "That's what we teach. You don't have to have lots of money to start with. You need to be able to pull in other people's money which is what accelerated Lee's route to wealth.

"And what a best gift that is to be able, like Lee and Jo have done, to give your kids the benefit of your personal development, education and knowledge. I can't wait till my son is 16, and I can say to him: I'm not going to give you any money, but I'll help you."

LEE AND JO'S TIPS

"Some people, when they're starting out, have a scattergun approach and try to do everything. You've just got to focus on one strategy."

"Keep going and never stop but make sure you get started!"

"Get round the right people. We're always motivated when we watch Samuel. It inspires us even now. That energy is so infectious."

"Networking is important. You need that injection of positivity and people who you can bounce ideas off."

"Property is a fantastic thing. You can actually scale it and scale it as quickly or slowly as you want to."

Chapter 7 – Joshua Robinson

Former chef makes tasty profits from rent-to-rents after losing £19,000 on Bitcoin

One-time chef Joshua Robinson lost £19,000 overnight in trading Bitcoin but recovered from that disastrous blow to become a rent-to-rent specialist, thanks to his training with Property Investors. He sells deals to investors, as well as earning thousands of pounds every month from five rent-to-rents under his control.

It is an incredible triumph for someone who left home at 16 and got caught up in the world of drugs before fatherhood made him realise he had to 'step up to the plate' to look after his child.

Joshua worked as a chef for seven years. He had a passion for it and worked his way up to become a head chef. Shifts of 14 to 16 hours, however, sucked the enthusiasm for the job out of him, combined with a paltry wage for the effort he put in.

There came a moment when it dawned on him that he needed to take charge of his own destiny and make a change in his life, he says.

"I stood in the kitchen one day and I was thinking I'm earning £350 this week for 45 hrs or more. That's just not good enough."

Joshua also objected to being dictated to by someone else. He yearned to be his own boss and to be able to provide for his family.

"I didn't want to live that life of going to work and being told when to eat and sleep. I just felt I couldn't do it. I didn't want to earn somebody else money and make them rich. I want to provide the best life I can for my children and build generational wealth, so their kids have no financial worries."

Describing himself as high functioning and capable of working 'ridiculously long days,' Joshua says he also has a hunger to succeed, having done well at school.

"I'm meant to do more than just work for somebody else for 40 hours a day for 40 years of my life, to then retire on 40 per cent to live out four years of the good life. It's not for me. People retire and that's usually when they die, not long after retiring because you stop using everything."

He adds: "It makes me feel sick thinking about going to do any job now. If I did that, I would never be happy again a day in my life."

Property investing seemed a natural choice for him to try his hand at because he had always had an interest in it from an early age.

"When I was younger and went on holiday, I would be looking at the buildings and loving the way they're designed. I've always had a fascination with property and wanting to get into it. I know there's good money to be made. The property market is never going anywhere. It's as safe as houses."

The young father-of-two laughs when recalling how Samuel's free YouTube content became his television because that was all he watched. He sat for hours at night, carefully going through all the videos and absorbing the valuable tips which would help him get started in property.

One of them was a *Winners on a Wednesday* interview with James Armstrong, a 21-year-old former electrician who had become a successful deal sourcer. Joshua vowed to himself that one day he would be the one being quizzed by Samuel Leeds and giving advice to other wannabe investors.

Another of the videos featured a 34-year-old man from his home town of Blackpool who was struggling with debt after being diagnosed with a rare stomach tumour. Glen Kirkham had attended one of Samuel's crash courses and so Samuel undertook a *Financial Freedom Challenge* with him. For seven days the multi-millionaire Property Investors founder lived with Glen and by the end of the week he had an income from real estate which covered his outgoings.

Joshua says he was 'gutted' that he had missed out on doing the challenge himself, but it reassured him that Samuel was really doing what he said he was doing.

"The fact he was willing to come to his house and help him was brilliant. I'd only just started watching him at that point. Seeing him do that with Glen, I thought this guy's amazing. He's helped turn him around.

"It confirmed to me that you can do this with the right training."

Joshua was still employed as a chef when he placed a trade on Bitcoin in 2018. He put it on in the morning and by dinnertime it was worth £19,000. Encouraged by his success, he put big lot sizes on but crucially with no stop loss to limit the maximum loss of a trade in the digital currency.

"It was a silly mistake. I fell asleep and woke in the morning to literally a couple of hundred pounds left in my account. It was like discipline your disappointment, don't cry over spilt milk. This was when I started looking into property because I needed to run a business and property was what I wanted to do."

From devouring all of Samuel's YouTube content, Joshua then enrolled on an online programme with Property Investors which gave him unlimited support.

"It was crazy value for money," he says. "You got the *Deal Finding Extravaganza* and *Never Use Your Own Money Again* [courses] on that and weekly coaching calls. You also got mentoring and could book in whenever you needed it. I was paying £95 a month. I would happily have paid that just for the mentoring."

Joshua also took part in the *Mastermind Forum* which allows members to get in touch with each other via Zoom to offer advice, share ideas and celebrate successes.

In addition to the course and the forum, he paid £500 to attend one of Samuel's *Discovery Days* and get help with his business plan. Joshua told this mentor that he was having trouble getting investors to commit to paying him a commission in his deal sourcing business.

'Straight up he called me a pussy and I was like, yes I am!"

He smiles at the recollection, but it proved to be a productive meeting.

"We went through how to approach it and what to say. I've not had an issue since."

Joshua was also introduced to Samuel's business mentor who advised him to concentrate on offering one kind of property deal. Consequently, Joshua now exclusively sources rent-to-rent opportunities, having gone into partnership with another property entrepreneur, Ed Harding. Together they have 'hit the ground running,' opening an office in Liverpool and employing two staff to help them run their business.

Joshua travels every day to the city from Blackpool. It takes him about an hour and ten minutes to get there but for him it is worth making the commute.

"I'm more efficient working in the office now. At home there's a lot more distraction and chance to procrastinate. You might say to yourself I need to go shopping for an hour. Then you've just lost an hour of your business, or I need to go to the gym, it's not busy. Then you've lost another two hours.

"Being around the right people and in the right environment is key to making a business."

Joshua merged his company, Prestige Sourcing, with his partner's firm and rebranded it as a new limited deal sourcing company called Robinson&Hardings.

All their rent-to-rents are in the North West, where their deal sourcing activities are concentrated predominantly, although they do offer a nationwide service.

They package and sell an average of four deals a month, charging a fee of £3,000 plus VAT for each one, or three per cent of the price of the property, whichever is the greater amount.

Their rent-to-rent properties in Liverpool are all offered as serviced accommodation on short lets, and they are about to take on another one in Salford.

"The ones in Liverpool are making a profit of between £700-900 a month. With the property we've just taken on we're looking at between £2,500 and £5,000 profit. On average, we're making £4,500 to £5,000 a month. With this one we're bringing on now that could double if we get it across the line."

They found their patch by accident after they began their search for property deals in the region and were put in contact with a management company. The furnished accommodation is mainly rented out to contractors who are working locally. They also cater for people moving house, who need somewhere to stay temporarily, along with travelling businessmen and women.

"You also have the tourists coming in for a weekend or night out. There's so much to do," Joshua points out.

As an entrepreneur who sells property investment deals, integrity is hugely important to him.

"Some of my investors have got hundreds of thousands of pounds to play with. Some have got £50,000 and worked hard for the last five years to save that, so you have to be thinking of these people all the time. You have to present the correct numbers.

"At the end of the day – as it has been said before – you can spend years building up your reputation and you can be destroyed in one fell swoop by one bad deal and it gets around.

'So, your integrity has to be there. You have to put yourself in their shoes. Would you be happy with somebody over-inflating the numbers and getting you to invest in a bad deal when you know the money is going to be lost? Me personally, I wouldn't sleep at night. I say this to my investors."

Education has been the cornerstone to giving him the confidence to look for properties his clients can buy. He has also had to learn how to calculate the return on investment and negotiate the price.

"When I set up my business, I wanted to have every understanding I possibly could. I never wanted to get to the point of having a conversation with an investor and not being able to answer a question or find a way around a problem. So, I did spend a long time making sure I got my education first. But you have to be careful you don't spend too much time educating yourself and never taking any action on it. Then that education is pointless."

Along with his job as a chef, Joshua also studied aerospace engineering until dropping out to do a business degree instead. He was taught, he says, by tutors who had never been in business themselves and nowadays only wants to be around people who are doing better than him in life.

The opposite was true when Joshua decided to leave home because he was constantly clashing with his father. He stayed in hostels and hung around with 'delinquents and degenerates' whose only aim in life was to find the money for drugs.

The birth of his first daughter when he was 18 made him veer away from that scene. The realisation that someone was dependent on him made him 'grow up.' She is now seven and he has another daughter aged three.

"I've changed now. I'm very anti all of that because I've seen what it does to people, and I've seen the path it's taken people down."

There have been hiccups along the way, Joshua admits, including times in the past when he has had to walk away from deals or offer refunds, but the future is looking promising. Influenced by the positivity in the Property Investors' community, he has set a high bar for what he wants to achieve.

His goal is to become a billionaire by expanding the company's portfolio of rent-to-rents and using the money from those to take on land developments. In the short-term, he plans to buy a house for his mother, who suffers from poor health, so that she no longer has to work long hours in her prison job.

After that, his target is to help his father and sisters, including building a house for one of them in nearby Morecombe. He would also like to provide places for the homeless to live, so that they have an address if they need to claim benefits until they find work and a permanent home.

Samuel says: "It's easy to judge people from where they've been, but actually it doesn't matter where they've been. What matters is where they're going. Joshua deserves massive congratulations. I look forward to seeing him continue to smash his goals in property going forward."

JOSHUA'S TIPS

"Go out there, educate yourself and take action – and keep going. There will be times when you fail, but it's never a failure. It's just a learning experience."

"I'm a council estate lad through and through. You can produce the life you want to produce for yourself with the right education. I'm sending my staff to Property Investors for rent-to-rent training."

"Samuel's YouTube content will educate you but there will be things you'll come up against that aren't on YouTube. The paid-for training gives you that extra push."

Chapter 8 – Tom Grierson

Property Investors helps teenager to earn more than some of his old teachers through rent-to-rents

Semi-professional rugby player Tom Grierson may only be 18 but in the year that he came of age he implemented every property strategy going, bar developing, to make himself financially free. He is even hoping to do that as well as he seeks to build on his success and create wealth for his family.

Just a few months after leaving school Tom was already earning more than some of his old teachers as a direct result of following the methods taught by Property Investors.

The teenager, who plays for Oldham RLFC, admits he still cannot believe he is making enough money never to have to work again, although he is far from ready to hang up his boots. On and off the field he is a hard worker with big ambitions.

It was Samuel Leeds' YouTube videos which got him hooked on the idea of earning a living from property while at the same time pursuing his sporting career.

"I managed to get away for a holiday and I just started scrolling on YouTube. I came across Samuel's videos and just binge-watched loads of them. I thought these are great. I didn't know you could do all these different type of things with property," Tom explains.

Aged just 17, he enrolled on a free online *Property Investors Crash Course* in February 2021 to find out more and was instantly captivated. The course lasted 10 hours and he was 'glued' to every single second of the stream.

It introduced him to all the creative strategies which can be used to generate high yields, including rent-to-rent. A fortnight later Tom secured his first rent-to-rent deal on a two-bedroom house in the Yorkshire town of Huddersfield after studying more of Samuel's videos on the subject.

It was on the market as a single let but Tom saw from the floor plan that there was a sitting room and a loft which could be converted into lettable rooms simply by putting beds in them.

Having researched his market, Tom worked out he could get £1,500 per month by turning it into a four-bed HMO. In return, he agreed to pay the landlord a guaranteed rent of £575 a month which was what it had been advertised at.

He sourced the beds and bedside tables from Ikea and decorated the house himself. His total outlay came to £1,000. This included the first month's rent of £575, which he paid on the day he signed the contract, and the paint and paintbrushes.

Tom avoided paying a deposit by pointing out that he would have to paint and furnish four rooms, as well as put a carpet in the loft.

"I explained what I wanted to do and said all of that didn't come cheap and they said yes, go for it."

It was a victory for persistence when Tom finally got the go ahead to rent out the property as a company let, having received around 30 rejections previously from agents.

"I spent a lot of time phoning agents who said we don't know what a company let is or a rent-to-rent. They would say: leave us alone and put the phone down, but I just kept going. The more times you ring the phone, the more likely you are to get a yes.

"I followed scripts of what I'd seen on Samuel's videos of what he'd done and how to talk to the agent. That kept me going."

Tom made sure he knew exactly what he was going to say before he called an agent and remained polite.

"It was fantastic when I eventually got a yes."

Tom's mother Ruth, who is a landlady herself, was worried when she discovered her son had rented a house after being on a Property Investors course. Her concern was that he might have trouble renting out the rooms and could be left with a liability on his hands.

"Her and my dad have done pretty well by buying properties, but only renting them out as single lets. She'd never heard of the concept of rent-to-rent.

"I told her I'd been on Samuel Leeds' online crash course and watched videos. It's a really good idea for someone of my age who doesn't have a lot of money or experience. I can make a few hundred pounds a month and I'll also get the experience of being a landlord.

"She said: 'I've never heard of this. I've been doing this for 20 years. I've got no idea what this is. Are you sure?' I said yeah, we'll figure it out."

His decision was vindicated when he quickly found tenants for the accommodation.

"It took two weeks to fill the rooms from when I picked up the keys and it made itself back in two months," he says.

Tom received no financial help from his parents to get started. Instead, he used his savings from doing odd jobs while at school to get himself launched. He also made use of OpenRent, SpareRoom and Facebook Marketplace to advertise his rooms for free.

"When the money first started coming in, I had to pinch myself. I've never heard of any other 18-year-old landlords. People were paying me to have a roof over their head. This was not the service I thought I'd be providing for people."

After the success of his initial venture, Tom was keen to find another deal, so reinvested the money he had made into advanced training with Property Investors.

His second coup was to clinch a lease option agreement on a property which he had spotted on Rightmove after searching for the oldest listed properties.

"The landlord had been trying to sell the property for a while, and it just wasn't budging at all. He'd also been renting the property for the past few years. The training teaches you that's the way you should look for properties – something that's been on the market for a while and then it's a bonus if it's been rented out before as well."

By having that information, it gave Tom a hint that whilst the owner wanted to sell, he did not need the money right then because he was open to the idea of it being rented out.

Explaining the lease option strategy, Tom says: "You agree to buy the property for a fixed price now, but you don't actually pay that. All you pay is on the option, which could be as little as £1, and you pay the landlord an agreed monthly fee.

"The property is worth around £200,000 and I agreed to buy it for £210,000 in 2028."

Up until that year he benefits from any capital appreciation and rent. If it has not increased in value, Tom can decide not to exercise his right to buy it.

"He has to sell it if I want to buy it, but I'm not obliged to buy which is the beauty of the deal."

That might seem unfair, Tom concedes. There are, however, clear advantages for the seller, he points out.

"The property is going to be completely off his hands for the next seven years. He's never going to have any arrears and he's not going to have to pay any major repairs. So, I'm completely taking care of the property for him."

Potentially the owner also gets his original asking price and more.

Tom furnished the property to a high standard and now rents it out as serviced accommodation on Airbnb and Booking.com. It is available for short staycations, as well as for contractors and people in between house moves who need somewhere to live temporarily.

It would rent out for £700 per month if there was just one tenant, he says, which is the same amount he pays the landlord.

"Last month it grossed around £3,000 and netted £1,750. That's after paying the cleaners and all the bills. For the rent-to-rent and lease option agreement I made a clean profit of £2,250 in one month."

Tom, who has become known as the 'property guy' in Huddersfield, where he is based, has also sourced a deal and completed a buy, refurbish, refinance project with a joint venture partner.

"I put some money into that and a lot of sweat equity. That was a property that was bought for £60,000 cash. We spent £10,000 on it and it's been revalued at £107,500. So, we can pull all our money out of that."

An 'innate hunger' to achieve more in property spurs him on, even though he could sit around doing nothing all day while the rent money keeps coming in.

"I may have to answer a few emails and messages, but I just want to do more and be in a position where I can do developments or maybe scale and systemise a sourcing company.

"With my age, and the time I've got and the people I've met, I really think the world's my oyster. I can put my mind into all the different strategies and put myself in a good position in 10 to 20 years' time."

His long-term aim is to build an empire so that his children in future and their children have the choice of not working. And he wants to make his business a family affair. He is already part way there. After seeing him succeed, his mother joined Property Investors' development course and his sister plans to take a year out from her university course to work with them both. Tom hopes his brother, who is an electrician, can also become involved when he sets up a construction company – one of his other goals.

Tom says that if a deal has fallen through, his mother has been there to pick him back up and both his parents, who run a lettings agency, have been 'sensational' in giving him advice and support.
He is grateful too for all the back-up he has received from the Samuel Leeds' community. Tom was 18 when he paid £1,000 for a Property Investors online deal sourcing course which he got back with interest by selling a deal. Later, when he could afford it, he became a fully-fledged member of the academy.

The training has fulfilled all his hopes: "Everything has been so informative. It's dotted every i and crossed every t. Without the training I wouldn't be where I am now. I'd be at university with everyone else partying. Instead,

I'm getting up at 6am to do viewings an hour away from where I live and making money."

Samuel, who also began his property career early in life, obtaining his first house at 17, says:

"It's a great buzz to see people winning in property. Some people will say Tom got lucky but actually Tom didn't get lucky. Tom created his own luck by putting himself at the right place at the right time. He went the right way about getting himself educated, studying the videos first and then signing up for paid training when he had made some money.

"That was smart, and he put a lot of work in, so credit where credit is due. What he's done is remarkable. A lot of 18-year-olds wouldn't even dream of taking the kind of action he's taken.

"It's not been easy. Tom's had lots of rejections but now he's financially free and he's achieved that so quicky. He's basically done almost every strategy that there is in the property industry. His experience is through the roof and he's making more money than some of his teachers when he was at school."

*Since Tom was interviewed for *Winners on a Wednesday*, he has gone on to turn over £100,000 on his rent-to-rent business and now controls seven properties. He says he owes Samuel Leeds a great debt on two accounts. "One, I've got a pretty well run SA business and also I met my girlfriend at one of Samuel's events in December 2021 and we're happier than ever just over a year on!"

TOM'S TIPS

"**If you're starting out with not much money, get educated. Go to a *Property Investors Crash Course* and look at what you might excel at. Then start calling agents and book viewings. As soon as you do that and get familiar with them, they'll say: I've seen this. This might be good for you** to start on."

"Don't get disheartened early on. It will happen and you will make the money. Once you get that first £300-400 from a rent-to-rent or that first couple of grand from a deal, you'll want to phone more agents and go on more viewings and then it will just snowball."

"If you pick up the phone without any confidence, it's really hard to get a conversation going with an agent. Make sure you know exactly what you're going to say."

"If you've not got that immediate support around you with family and friends talk to someone at the crash course and then you could even do a deal together."

Chapter 9 – Osita Eze

Investor threw away his TV so he could 'channel' all his energy into property

Hundreds of people have made new lives for themselves thanks to the training Samuel Leeds and his coaches deliver. As a committed Christian, the multi-millionaire founder of Property Investors feels compelled to help others improve their situation by sharing his knowledge. As he puts it:

"We're on a mission to help people have the finances to live the life they deserve. This is having a positive rippling effect across the world and across people's hearts and lives."

Osita Eze certainly felt this feel-good effect when he came to a two-day *Property Investors Crash Course* in London in October 2019.

He says: "There was an ambience of positivity. I'd never seen such an environment. It sparked something in me that was asleep. Since then, it hasn't stopped."

After the crash course Osita sprang into action, signing up for the academy straight away to learn more about property investing. Since then, he has built up a portfolio of six rent-to-rent serviced accommodation apartments which make him an average profit of £3,000 a month. A few months ago, he also embarked on his first buy, refurbish, refinance project.

For someone who has gone through some very challenging experiences it is quite a turnaround.

The Nigeria-born entrepreneur experienced poverty growing up and went through the horror of seeing people dying in front of him. It fuels his ambition now to reach a position where he can leave a legacy for his four children as well as do something to help his fellow countrymen.

Osita, who also has a full-time job as an engineer, says he enjoys his work but when he came to the UK in 2010 it was with 'a notion of getting into business.'

"I had a vision to leave a legacy for my family and to join hands with good Africans who are trying to help Africa regain its potential," he explains.

"I was born into a family where from childhood I knew what it means to be wretched. I've seen people die in situations that are avoidable. People have died in my hands and the pain of the fact these deaths are avoidable has been living with me since childhood.

"I've always been set on this path to leave a legacy that will help us, my immediate community and my people in Africa to live a better life. So that has been my drive beyond me doing this for my wife and my children. The greater African situation is the major drive for everything I do."

When Osita came to this country, he knew nothing about property and in fact was put off having anything to do with it after discovering that to buy a house people took out a mortgage 'till they die'

"I was never saving to buy a property. At some point my wife said let's buy a property. I said no, I want a business that will help me live the life I want to live. If I want to buy a property, I'll buy it and pay it off. I don't like to owe people."

Before landing his present job, Osita found himself jumping from one employer to the next to gain a modest wage rise. He also became frustrated by not having enough time for himself and his family. So, he started searching for ways to make money alongside his job.

He tried his hand at a variety of enterprises, including buying cars at auction, doing them up and then selling them. Lack of time, however, again proved to be a problem.

"I wasn't having time to do it properly. People might want to view a car and I would be at work, so that affected the business."

As a result, he was forced to close it and was out of pocket through having to sell five cars at half price.

Undaunted, Osita, who lives just outside London, partnered with a friend to register an oil and gas exploration company, making several attempts to secure wells in Aberdeen.

"It's not a cheap vision. We pursued it for about a couple of years. Again, that didn't work out. I got burnt on that one as well," he recalls.

Whilst all his efforts to make a go of a business misfired, deep down he was convinced something would happen to improve his situation, although he had no idea how it would come about.

It was the arrival of a new employee at his office which turned out to be the harbinger of change. They became friends and over lunch would have 'positive and constructive' discussions.

"We would ask ourselves: 'Who are these people with big cars who have time for their families? There must be something they're doing that we're not doing.'

His friend lent him his copy of *Rich Dad Poor Dad* by Robert Kiyosaki which got him thinking.

"I remember coming back from work reading that book on the train and got to where Robert Kiyoski started talking about property. At that page I put a stop and I said: 'I need to take action.'

"When I read that book, I began to see the possibility of a life in property."

Having decided that this could be a career for him, Osita set about finding a trainer which led to him attending a free crash course on a Saturday. He took his young daughter along to introduce her to the industry from an early age.

Osita got some good information from the event, but felt it was lacking in other ways.

"I'm a very passionate person. If there is not enough positive energy, I don't easily connect and I felt these guys couldn't take me to where I wanted to be. They gave me the knowledge, but it would just dissolve like ice.

"So, I searched on YouTube for property trainers in the UK and Samuel Leeds popped up. I saw he had loads of videos and thought he must be doing something right to have all these videos. I clicked on one and he almost jumped on my face. His energy was like BOOM!"

After that Osita attended the *Property Investors Crash Course* and then enrolled on the academy.

"The good thing about the crash course and the academy is it gives you that environment to thrive," he says.

Osita used his credit card to pay the fee for the year-long academy programme, but with dependents in Britain and Nigeria, and no guarantee he would get rich, it was a risky step.

"When I started out in property, I didn't have any money. I had to borrow from people and just pray that it worked and put my all into it. I wanted to do it so badly."

If it did not work out, he was prepared to shoulder the blame.

"I believe that every adult should be able to take responsibility for the decisions they make. It was my decision to do it and I have to take responsibility. When people take decisions and look for who to blame [if something goes wrong] I don't think it's right.

"I lost a lot of money with my other businesses, but I didn't start blaming anyone. I ventured into those businesses. I didn't consult anyone. That's part of my history and the decisions I've taken in life, but I gained a lot of experience and strengths."

Osita is grateful to his wife for organising their home life so that he could concentrate on the training.

He describes the Property Investors Academy as 'a wonderful place' populated by positive-minded students who are full of energy, chasing one goal to succeed, and with big hearts to help each other. This is true also for the trainers, who are always there to offer support, he points out.

A few months into the academy, Osita confided in his mentor Samuel that he was struggling to find the time to go on property viewings. So, they drew up a plan to solve the problem.

Osita still has the piece of paper on which it was written.

"That plan was a gamechanger. I understood every strategy and started trying all of them. Samuel told me to choose one for cashflow that suited my circumstances. I said serviced accommodation and he said put all your energy there."

His initial deal came quickly after that. Samuel became his first guest which gave him the encouragement to ramp up his business. He took two months' leave without pay and during this period secured four more rent-to-rents.

Under the agreement, he pays the flat owners a guaranteed rent each month and then lets out the accommodation for short stays, charging a higher rate.

Three of the furnished apartments are in Birmingham, one is in Staines close to Heathrow Airport and another one is next to Windsor Castle. The sixth unit is a former church in Portsmouth which was converted into duplex apartments.

The profit fluctuates from month to month, depending on the time of year, but Osita says it can be as much as £6,000. Rent-to-rent appealed to him as a strategy because he regarded it as having less risk in terms of capital involvement.

"If I were to buy a house in some of the areas where I offer serviced accommodation, I'd be spending thousands and thousands of pounds. But with less than £8,000 you have a decent serviced accommodation business that is able to give you a wonderful return on investment. You're controlling another person's property and you're making cashflow. So, for me control is more interesting than owning a property.

"There's no magic to it. It's just there's a lot of work involved and if you're not trained you can't do it. It's a tough business. There are a lot of things you have to do to make it work. If you don't know how to do them, you can just as well forget it. If you don't have the right skills for it and the right team in place you will lose your deposit."

He was tempted to give up his job, as even his average monthly takings of £3,000 made him financially independent. Samuel, however, advised him to build up his income first because of his family commitments and the fact that takings can fall in the low season.

It was good advice but hard to take when he is pumped up with enthusiasm.

"The fire in my belly is so hot I'm the only one who understands it. At the same time, I'm being careful how I move. I don't want to be driven by emotion. I'm taking my time."

Osita is relentless in pursuing his passion, viewing properties in the evenings and working late into the night on his property dealings.

"Sometimes if I work in the office, I finish around 6 o'clock and come back around 8 or 9. I switch back to property. I work to 3am. Sometimes I do this seven days a week without enough sleep. It is tough but if you keep your eye on the ball where you want to get to, your mind will work alongside your body."

He even got rid of his television at home to keep himself focused.

His punishing schedule is reaping rewards. His last deal saw him joint venture with another academy member to tackle a buy, refurbish, refinance project – a strategy he learnt about during his training.

Osita snapped up a house at auction for £72,000 and is in the process of carrying out the refurbishment which will cost an estimated £20,000 to £25,000. He and his partner acquired the property with a bridging loan. A chartered valuer has given them a valuation of £120,000 once the work is finished. This will enable them to refinance the mortgage and pull out all but £10,000 of their money to reinvest in another scheme.

"That is a benefit of being in the academy. You meet people who want to invest and if it's the right deal they want to work with you."

Osita is grateful to Samuel Leeds and his team for all their assistance in developing him into a successful entrepreneur. On one occasion, he and his business partner were about to buy a house when the price went up at the last minute. Samuel advised them not to fork out the extra money.

"I really loved the support he gave me then because I didn't believe anything like that would happen. We were close to exchanging and then they said they needed extra money. That just rocked the deal. We had spent some money on it and wondered whether we should still go for it but as Samuel says you're not buying a house to live in. It's an investment and it's about formulas, not feelings.

"My mindset has changed too. Before the crash course if I spent £1 on my credit card, I would pay it back. I refused to increase my credit card limit. All this has changed and I'm seeing my vision coming true."

Samuel is full of admiration for his student: "Osita was in a situation where it would have been very easy for him to say I can't do this but the first time I met him I knew he would be successful because he has great energy and works so hard. He lights up a room when he comes into it and pulls everybody up. He also has great belief which is important.

"The fact he's managed to replace his income on top of a very demanding, full-time job as an engineer is quite remarkable."

OSITA'S TIPS

"Don't waste time. Just take a leap from the cliff and develop your wings on your way down."

"Get trained and believe in yourself. Everything you can conceive and believe works."

"Everything happens in your mind. Get your mindset right and pursue any dream you have in your head. The world is waiting for you."

"Sometimes it is good to pause if you know you're not getting to where you deserve to be. Check what is impacting you."

"The biggest thing I've learnt through the academy is with the right people around you everything is possible."

Chapter 10 – Darcy Burgoyne

'Failure not an option' for investor who gave up a top job to build rent-to-rent portfolio

High-flier Darcy Burgoyne's friends and family were shocked when she gave up a paid degree apprenticeship at one of the world's biggest investment banks to go into property. Her shocked parents wondered why their teenage daughter would want to sacrifice the prospect of a lucrative career.

What they did not realise, says Darcy, who now makes a healthy living from rent-to-rents, is that she was unhappy. She was working full-time while also having to learn about stocks and shares at university.

"I don't tend to tell people how I feel. I'm very closed off. Had they known how I felt for months I think they would have been different.

"I felt awful, depressed. You just wake up and do the same routine and you look forward to the weekend. The weekend comes and goes really quickly, and you just dread the next working week. It was just a vicious cycle. Lockdown made it worse because I couldn't even look forward to my weekends."

The coronavirus pandemic triggered her decision to leave after she had been watching Samuel Leeds' YouTube videos and set her mind on becoming a property entrepreneur.

"I always knew when my degree finished, I wanted to go into property but then during the pandemic I thought why wait, I know I can do it. So, I did a couple of free courses and then I paid for the advanced training."

It was during a group chat on the *Financial Freedom Intensive course* that she revealed she wanted to ditch her job, having enrolled on the online version of the Property Investors Academy.

Samuel, who was in on the Zoom call, advised her against taking this step, worried that Darcy, who was then 19, could find herself out of work and in debt if she failed to make it in property. Many Property Investors students go on to become financially independent, but as with any type of training there is no guarantee of success. Hard work and persistence are also required.

In Darcy's mind, failure was never an option, so she went ahead anyway, handing in her resignation in May 2021.

"I'm very confident in myself and I knew if I quit then I would have no other choice but to be successful. I don't really believe in failure because I think in life you are taught something and then you put it into action," she explains.

During lockdown, Darcy was living at home which enabled her to pay the academy fee from her wages before she left and still have some savings.

It turned out well for her, despite everyone's concerns. On the *Serviced Accommodation Intensive* course, she was able to meet Samuel and set up her first deal.

"That was the best thing ever because we could go in person. I do believe environment is everything, especially if you're new. You can meet people who've done it and you see success in the flesh, so you believe it a lot more.

"We made phone calls to agents, and I managed to get a viewing for an apartment in Portsmouth which was brilliant. This was on the training after we'd been taught everything and given the scripts of what to say. That phone call later turned into my first deal."

Darcy proved to be a skilled operator from the start. With no job or references to her name, and zero income, she still persuaded the landlord to agree to a rent-to-rent arrangement. She even negotiated a discount on the rent. In return, she is allowed to rent out the flat as serviced accommodation and make a profit on it by charging a higher rate than what she pays to the landlord.

"I used all the advantages of it being a company let. It's guaranteed rent [for the landlord]. Someone can hold you accountable which, for the landlord, was very appealing because with a tenant it's very hard to hold them responsible and get any money back. But it's different with a company and I just explained all those benefits.

"They had dealt with company lets before which really helped because they knew what it was."

The owner had hoped to achieve a rent of £1,150 a month for the small two-bed apartment near Gunwharf Quays, but Darcy managed to haggle down the price to £1,075. The difference funds her Wi-Fi and electricity bill each month.

And visitors are queuing up to book the apartment for short stays, she says.

"I secured it in June 2021 and the profit on average is about £700 a month which I'm really happy with because it's a cheap rent in a great location. In a good month it's £1,000. I would be making more but I pay for private parking for my guests as I know how much of a nightmare parking can be in a city centre.

"I have to pay £130 a month for it but it's worth it because then I don't get guests saying I had the hassle of trying to park."

That first deal bolstered Darcy's confidence, consolidating what she had learnt on the training and what she knew she could achieve.

"The first is the hardest. Once you have one you have something to leverage when you're going to get number two because you can say I can give you a landlord reference, or I got this one through another agent and this is how they did it."

Even though many people thought Darcy was 'crazy' to relinquish her hard-won apprenticeship, her partner Ben backed her.

"The only person who truly supported me was Ben because he knew if I wanted to do something I was going to do it. My family, as much as they love and support me, didn't understand it. I'm not from a rich background. They thought I was on a good path with the bank and had a secure job.

"But I am not about security. You only get one life, so why not have fun with it?"

Despite her parents' apprehensions, her father acted as a guarantor for her first rent-to-rent agreement, for which she is grateful. However, he made it clear he did not want to be a guarantor a second time.

Just like her attitude to failure, it was simply 'not an option' for that to be a stumbling block, so Darcy pressed on and secured another rent-to-rent agreement. This one is a two-bedroom house in Winchester with a view of the cathedral from the balcony. In the first two days of renting it out on Airbnb in November 2021, bookings worth £2,500 came in and are still rolling in 'thick and fast.'

Based on an occupancy rate of 75 per cent and a nightly charge of £200 to £400, depending on the time of year, her forecast is that it will generate an average, monthly profit of £2,000 and £3,000. During peak times, such as the summer and university graduation days, her occupancy rate rises to 90 per cent.

Just from these two properties Darcy expects to earn more than she was making in her banking job which paid her £22,000 a year.

"Also, I don't have to work 12 hours a day being bored to get it, which is the best thing. I love painting and decorating and choosing interior designs which is why I love serviced accommodation. I can do it on my laptop while I'm watching *Friends*. That's my job.

"My sister asked me the other day where I was going. I said I've got to go to Ikea. That's part of my job now. She went no. I said: 'actually it is.' My job description probably is, go to Ikea to get furniture!"

Whilst Samuel says she has a way of making everything look easy and seamless, there have been challenges to overcome. Darcy received a lot of rejections from agents before clinching her second deal but persisted because she knew Winchester was an affluent area, with 'gorgeous' properties, a university and high nightly rates for short stay accommodation.

She hooked the deal by directly negotiating with the landlord, who is a wealthy lawyer based in Dubai, rather than going through an agent.

Darcy pays the owner £1,550 per month for the house which has many old features including massive ceilings, beautiful windows and a kitchen with an island and a dining table.

"When it comes to serviced accommodation, it's all about what can you offer that's unique. No one wants to come from their boring grey/beige home to another boring beige/grey home."

The property, which has the added attraction of being close to a popular market, was filled with junk when she took it on, so the landlord was happy for her to do it up and rent it out at a profit. She painted and furnished it herself with bargain buys from Facebook Marketplace, spending £2,500 to create a high-end look. She also provided quality linen and had to pay two months' rent plus a deposit as security, but no guarantor was required this time, thanks to her successful pitch.

There is so much more to managing serviced accommodation than just putting it on Airbnb and waiting for the bookings to come in, Darcy emphasises.

"You need the training because there are tiny things you would never think you have to worry about, then they come up and you do. Even like bin collections. You can't ask your guests to put your bin bags out. Someone's got to be responsible for it."

If something does go wrong, then that can result in bad reviews and lost bookings unless you remedy the situation quickly, she says. There are other pitfalls to look out for too, like avoiding double bookings and learning to have systems in place to ensure the linen is dealt with properly.

Her first few months in property have just been a 'taster session,' the 20-year-old insists as she sets her sights on extending her portfolio of rent-to-rents and joining the elite multi-millionaire club.

Darcy concedes she had 'a perfect life' in one sense and can see in hindsight why her parents were so concerned.

"I was being paid to do a degree at 18-years-old. Only the top one per cent got into the job, so a lot of people were very questioning of my decisions. But I just think with degrees nowadays unless you need it what's the point? I'd rather start property now and be successful than wait to finish my degree and look back with regret."

She also felt she could afford to take a risk because she had no responsibilities, such as having children or a mortgage and bills to pay.

These days her life is far more flexible, and she enjoys every day, not just weekends. She can choose her hours which allows her to see her family and friends when she is not working on her property business.

Her average day, when preparing a serviced accommodation property, consists of booking a slot at the local tip to dispose of any unwanted items, having a takeaway for dinner and then going home and sleeping.

"If I'm not renovating a house, then I wake up, go to the gym, maybe go for a forest walk, have some nice lunch, then make my agent calls, and sift through my emails to see if there are any bits and bobs I need to order. Then I cook a nice dinner, sit with my family and just chill. It's a nice life."

Her father still tells her to be careful, but she is philosophical about it.

"My dad is the most risk averse person you'll ever meet. I think if I bought him a nice fishing boat he'd stop telling me that! One day perhaps."

Samuel is impressed by what his young trainee has achieved: "I think Darcy is going to inspire a lot of people because she's been able to gain financial freedom at such a young age and so quickly. Her results at her age are not typical. She's also a naturally confident, good negotiator. She negotiated a sofa down from £2,000 to £800. I'm so proud to see her doing well."

DARCY'S TIPS

"Just take the risk and take the action."

"Don't expect results overnight. You have to actually put in work. It doesn't just come."

"There will be a lot of no's on the phone, awkwardness and disappointment, but once you get that one yes you will forget all those horrible phone calls."

"Don't moan or make excuses. Get networking even if you feel a bit awkward."

"Sometimes it would get to me seeing other students earning £10,00 a month after three months when I was working so hard and not even close to that. But then I would have Samuel's weekly call or a call with a mentor and they would remind me to take it at my own pace. I realised I needed to stop comparing myself."

Chapter 11 – Kamil Domski

100 'no's' can't could not stop investor becoming financially free

It would take most people years to become financially free through building up a buy-to-let portfolio. As Samuel Leeds points out, the average investor needs to save for the deposit before they can purchase another rental property and that can take a long time.

Even when they do buy a house, the returns are minimal compared to other forms of investment and then there are management costs, maintenance and voids which eat away at their profits. And yet that for many remains the traditional route to wealth through lack of awareness of other strategies.

Family man Kamil Domski was one such investor. His property journey started in 2015 when he and his wife bought their house. Two years later they pulled out some of the equity and topped it up with savings to acquire a buy-to-let property. It then took them until 2020 to save enough money to buy their second one.

It was at this point that it dawned on Kamil that they would need a lot of buy-to-lets to create a level of income sufficient to cover all their bills.

"I started thinking there must be a quick way of getting financially free. Buy-to-lets are great but it takes time to save a deposit and then buy another house and set it up and so on. This was why I came across Samuel's videos and realised there were different strategies which I wanted to explore."

He decided to try renting out HMOs and paid to do some training with Property Investors. Afterwards Kamil took the bold step of giving up his job as a production engineer to become a full-time entrepreneur and joined the Property Investors Academy a few months later.

It was Christmas Eve 2020 and Kamil was eager to gain more knowledge. He also wanted to benefit from the academy network and the chance to meet other investors. It did the trick. Within a year he had four rent-to-rents in Coventry which would earn him as much, if not more than he was making before.

There was another advantage too. The 34-year-old father-of-one estimated he would only need to work about half a day a week on managing his portfolio. With the rest of his time, he could focus on more advanced strategies to increase his cashflow.

Kamil is now well on his way to achieving the life of independence he always envisaged for himself He earned around £2,000 a month as a production engineer in the aerospace industry but yearned for change.

"It was a very good job. I started as a quality inspector and went to college in the meantime. I progressed my way through the company and that was great. But that wasn't taking me to where I wanted to be.

"My dream is not to have to work. I want to have a choice rather than the duty to go somewhere and do something for somebody else," Kamil explains.

Even so, with a five-year-old son to look after, it was a big decision to leave his job. He says his wife supported him which made it possible.

"Massive gratitude goes to my wife because I wouldn't have been able to achieve this without her. My wife is working part time but also running her own business. We worked out we had enough income from my wife's business to cover our living expenses and I could focus on this business full time. I gave myself about six months to see what the result would be."

Kamil tried to sell property deals while he was still working but found that with his other commitments having to make calls and visit estate agents was too time-consuming. He decided to recalibrate his business and concentrate on securing a rent-to-rent HMO deal which would require less active involvement once it was set up.

Aware that he had set himself a deadline of six months to succeed, Kamil wasted no time in looking for an opportunity. He had already lined up his first deal while serving his notice period. But then he encountered a problem. Two days before he picked up the keys to the property the landlord informed him that his lender did not permit sub-letting.

The alarm bells started ringing in his head. It was July 2021, and he was about to leave his employment with no deals under his belt. So, he immediately set about finding another rent-to-rent agreement, following the process his trainers had taught him on the academy.

"I was ringing and sending messages and religiously doing that every single day. My wife was laughing because I was getting up in the morning, doing my daily routine and dressing up like I was going to work in a shirt and sitting by the desk. I was taking it that this was my full-time time job right now. So, if I treated it seriously it would pay off."

Kamil lost count of how many rejections he had but says it felt like a least 100 'no's' before he finally got a 'yes' on a property the following month.

"Most of the time it was, I'm sorry we don't do that, or the figure is not satisfactory, or we do that ourselves. I understand that was part of the process – go for no. Samuel says that in the training. I was going for that no because I knew every single no was taking me closer to that yes.

"Samuel teaches that if you follow the process, you will get the result you need."

Whilst Kamil was disappointed to see his first deal fall through, it taught him a valuable lesson. He now points out to landlords that it is their contractual responsibility to check if there are any restrictions on renting out their property.

He also sends the owner his terms and conditions before they sign an agreement to ensure both parties are happy with it.

"I say read it and have a think about it because it's going to be binding for three to five years so it's very important that you understand what you're signing. Make sure you're OK with it and I am OK with it, and this is where we can make a business together."

Through his management company, Kamil pays the owners of the four rent-to-HMOs which he controls a set, guaranteed monthly rent. He also looks after the properties with his maintenance team. In return, he is allowed to rent out the accommodation at a higher rate to make a profit.

In total, he has 21 rooms under his control which, when fully occupied, give him a monthly income slightly above what he was earning before.

"My minimum goal is to achieve £500 from a rent-to-rent deal. This is something Samuel teaches. I remember that from the *Rent-to-Rent Intensive*. I'm trying to be conservative with my numbers as well as calculating the bills. I prefer to make more money accidentally than less money because I didn't take that into account in the first place. That's my absolute minimum."

The house was being managed for the landlord by someone who had other properties and was happy to pass this one to Kamil. He had to put down a deposit of £1,700 to get the keys to his first property but it needed no work doing on it.

"It was in such great condition that I didn't have to pay a single penny to refurb the property. I wanted to have it as my first one. That was like my little pearl."

With a subsequent deal, he avoided having to give the landlord any money until the first tenant moved in.

"I was meant to pick up the keys three weeks earlier. Unfortunately, the jobs which needed to be done on the property weren't finished. The landlord said he was happy for me to have the keys so I could set up some viewings. However, we wouldn't be able to move in tenants until a certain time because there was still snagging (checks on building work) going on.

"I said how about I pay you when I move in my first tenant? We both thought that was fair."

Students who join the year-long Property Investors Academy programme are encouraged to make live calls so that they learn through doing.

Kamil says he loves that aspect of the training.

"It's not just about sitting there for two or three days listening to your mentors. It's all about seeing how they do it live. Then you do it yourself. There were people in the room on the day saying they'd got viewings and deals booked. It was absolutely incredible. If you have a room full of 60 people and all of them are sharing something, then you're absorbing it. That's the beauty of the academy and the live events because it becomes part of you as well."

All the other people in his group on the Property Investors Academy have also gone on to secure deals and become financially independent.

"It's normal," says Kamil. "People who pay that much money commit to something. That's why this room is full of people who want to get to something and that's the beautiful thing. Even if you wanted to be lazy, it's impossible because they infect you with their activeness and you want to become the same."

When his properties are fully tenanted, Kamil's income is largely passive. There are inspections, safety checks and administration which need to be done but this takes up a fraction of his time. Sitting back and doing nothing, has never been an option. From the start he realised this freedom would enable him to look at ways of expanding business through house flips and buy, refurbish, refinance projects. He is also keen to build a portfolio of properties which he owns.

His wife is 'super happy' with what he has achieved so far.

"Every morning we wake up and say let's go for more. So, we motivate ourselves. She's also running her own business. We try to keep the mindset very positive. I think we're getting better and better at it."

Kamil adds: "The reason I went into property is my family. I want them to be financially free and have choice."

Samuel's charity work in Africa has also inspired him to help others less fortunate than himself once he no longer needs to worry about his cashflow. As Kamil explains, he wants to share the fruits of his labour in future.

"When you're starting to think about doing something bigger in your life, I say don't just think about yourself. Think about others. One change in your life can make so many changes in other people's lives. That's what I believe should be a driving force for many other people."

Summing up Kamil's attributes as a property entrepreneur, Samuel says: "It's so important to have belief, otherwise you can decide not to take action because you think something is too good to be true. Kamil has had belief and has acted on it. That's why he's doing really well.

"Sometimes people think if they get a recurring passive income of £2,000-

£3,000 a month they'll just lie on a beach and do nothing, but actually that's just phase one. Phase one is replacing your income and becoming financially free. The next phase is building up wealth for your family, security, leaving generational legacies, setting up charities and really making a big impact. Now Kamil is moving towards that stage and that's exciting."

KAMIL'S TIPS

"Training is a must. You can't pretend you're a super pro rent-to-renter without taking the training."

"Training will give you a lot of knowledge but if you're not prepared to change your mindset and believe in yourself that training will be in vain."

"Think if others can do it I can as well."

"Establish a daily routine. I listen to motivational speeches so that I set my day on the right path."

"Surround yourself with people who are successful and doing what you're doing. Joining the Property Investors Academy helps you do that. I'm in touch every day with people I can brainstorm with."

"Celebrate every little thing you achieve in life."

"It's important to have a mentor. I had one-to-one calls on the academy with a mentor who helped me with my business plan."

Chapter 12 – Simon Olsen

Engineer clocks up £80K from his first deal after joining Property Investors Academy

Hard work defines Simon Olsen. He is the type of person who has to be busy. It is why he has managed to successfully combine a career as an engineer and a property entrepreneur. He enjoys his day job as a manager as much as his sideline making money from bricks and mortar.

"You ask my partner. I'm terrible when I'm bored. I just annoy everyone. I need to be doing something," he says.

Being a 'grafter' in life has certainly paid off for Simon who is making a small fortune from buying investment properties in his spare time after going into business with his father. His first deal after joining the Property Investors Academy netted £80,000. Since then, he has taken on more money-spinning ventures, including a converted chapel on a beach which will be rented out to holidaymakers.

It all began for Simon a few years ago when he was made redundant and received a lump sum which he wanted to invest. Property had always interested him, so in 2016 he bought a derelict, three-bedroom, semi-detached house.

As Simon describes it, "At the time I had no real property knowledge or understanding of different strategies. I thought the best thing to do was buy a house, fix it and sell it for a profit."

His father agreed to come in with him 50-50 and they set about renovating the house themselves. Simon by now had found a new job as an engineer and his father was also working full-time. It took them a year, therefore, to complete the project, but their efforts were rewarded in the end.

"We purchased the property for £250,000 and made £70,000 on it when we sold it," says Simon.

With this success under their belts, it would have been a natural step to repeat the process with another house. It was not until 2020, however, that Simon touched property again. In the intervening years, he went back to university to take a degree in business.

"I wanted to diversify. I think I've always been interested in business as well. It helped me with my career but also gave me a platform into property to understand the business side of it – how to set up a company, do the accounts, strategy, planning, project management. It covered it all.

"The business degree was sponsored by the company. I paid with my time by studying for it at the weekend."

Around this time Simon also started watching some of Samuel Leeds' YouTube videos on property investing. Simon was friends with two of his former students, Darren Andrews and Ella Attrill, of Della Estates, who trained with the academy and became property millionaires in just eight months.

"I used to go to school with Darren. I saw their *Winners on a Wednesday* interview with Samuel. They were a real inspiration. Some of the projects they've done are massive."

Having seen how well they had done, Simon enrolled on the training with Property Investors in 2020. It was all online as the live events had been suspended due to Covid restrictions. So, he 'indulged' himself in learning about all the various strategies for making money out of real estate.

With so much information at his fingertips about HMOs, serviced accommodation, rent-to-rents and deal sourcing, Simon wondered what to do with it all. So, he chose to go down the route of finding an HMO deal. But when an opportunity presented itself, he was unable to obtain a mortgage because of his lack of experience as a landlord.

Simon recognises now, with the benefit of being trained, that had he not sold the first investment house which he and his father refurbished, then lenders might not have rejected his application.

"Looking back on that one in 2016 I should have kept it and rented it out or I could have refinanced it and pulled the money out."

More frustration followed when Simon decided to go back to his previous strategy of 'flipping' properties. He found another three-bedroom, semi-detached house which was already being done up. The builder, who owned it, had been carrying out an extensive renovation, including a loft conversion and moving some walls downstairs. Halfway through the work, he put it up for sale. Seizing his chance, Simon made a 'cheeky offer' which was accepted, only for the builder to pull out at the last minute.

"That was a lesson for me. I learnt you can't always win in property," says Simon philosophically.

He also remembered something else he had been taught – that property entrepreneurs cannot become emotionally attached. They need to keep a cool head.

"Samuel says never be at ease until you've got the keys. I think that is so true."

Recovering from this setback, Simon put in more offers on properties, all of which were rejected, but kept going until eventually one was accepted. As the saying goes, 'If at first you don't succeed, try, try again.' So, Simon resorted to his tried and tested formula. He identified another three-bed semi which could be improved and sold at a profit.

This one hardly needed any work doing on it apart from requiring a fresh lick of paint and some tidying up. The purchase price in 2020 was £250,000 and the sale went through smoothly.

"At the time I didn't know about bridging finance, raising capital or angel investors. So, I put a mortgage on it and did the refurb on it. The property is now worth £330,000."

After that he learnt how to recycle his cash, using the buy, refurbish, refinance, rent method to raise funds for further investments.

"When we remortgage that one early next year, we can pull a big lump out of it. There's hardly any money left in the deal."

The 'chapel on the beach' is a departure from his usual strategy. He submitted an offer of £237,000 for the building which was accepted. Unlike, his other properties, this one had already been fully refurbished and converted into a two-bedroom house with a new kitchen and a bathroom. The plan is to turn the property, which comes with a 999-year lease, into a holiday let.

"We're looking to push it through quickly. It's in a prime location – the beach is your garden – and has all the period features, glass windows and beams. It also has a storeroom. For serviced accommodation you want something unique. So, I think we could turn that into a kids' cave or a storage area for kite surfers."

To get a mortgage Simon had to ask two independent companies to give him a low, medium and high valuation of how much it could be rented out for. Even the lowest estimate would generate a healthy income.

"In the high season we're looking at £1,200 to £1,300 a week. In the low season it's around £650 to £750. They're really good numbers."

He adds: "Our income at the moment is around £2,500 per month. That's from the three-bed we've got, an HMO and one of the flats we're refurbishing."

The four-bedroom HMO is compliant with fire doors and meets all the other regulations for shared accomodation. The rooms are spread over three storeys and there is the potential to create another bedroom. However, the rooms are not yet being rented out. This is because Simon and his father came to the rescue of a couple from their area who needed somewhere to live after their house was struck by lightning.

"They were looking for somewhere to rent short-term just so they could be close to their kids' school. It was the perfect location for them. We agreed they could have it for 12 months. We hadn't finished it. We were just about to furnish it.

"We could definitely get more money for it as an HMO but in this business, it can't just be about money. It has to be about people as well and how we can give something back to our community."

Simon became a member of the full Property Investors Academy after completing the online courses. It gave him access to the 'best' power team in the industry, including trainers, mentors and mortgage brokers, as well as a network of people to do deals with. He was also able to hear about their strategies and learn from them.

"It's like a family of property investors and there's so much energy at the live events," he says.

At one point Simon worried about how he would be able to carry on his daytime work while also trying to scale his property business.

"To do that I was very fortunate that my dad decided to join the business with me. He is very much looking after the day-to-day operations and all the maintenance which is really good. That allows me to focus on not only my full-time job but on finding new deals and opportunities."

Simon also has a supportive partner. When he is not at work, he and his dad share the task of improving properties.

"We tend to be hands-on. All the refurbs we just about do ourselves, apart from the gas and the electrics."

His favourite scheme to date is the ongoing development of a block of two maisonettes. They purchased the block for £300,000 and have finished the refurbishment of the top one. The rent per unit will be £1,000 a month, with the first one about to be let out.

With a projected spend of just over £60,000 and an end value of about £440,000, that will again produce a profit of £80,000 – plus a rent of £2,000 coming in each month. They also own the freehold and intend to split the titles.

"Russell (Samuel Leeds' brother and business partner) has kindly given me the details of a solicitor. That's part of having that power team being on the academy."

The father and son duo are also looking at acquiring some land with a derelict building on it which is being sold for £500,000. Their plan would be to divide the building into two separate units, each worth around £600,000, which would give them a huge yield.

Simon's reason for going into property was to build long-term wealth and stability for his family and he is well on his way to achieving that aim.

Serviced accommodation appeals to him more than HMOs now, he says, because it provides an opportunity to be creative and 'do something unique,' as with the chapel, compared to just renting out a bedroom.

Similarly, he prefers the BRR strategy over taking on a buy-to-let as it releases money for more investments over and over again. It also gives him the satisfaction of taking the 'worst house and turning it into the best house on the street' which is what he is doing with the maisonettes. And capital appreciation excites him more than cashflow because he earns well as an engineer.

Despite gloomy predictions that property prices are going to fall, he remains optimistic about the future.

"I just can't see it happening, especially in this country. There may be certain areas where it does. There's a housing shortage. All the properties I've had have rented out before we've even advertised."

Samuel is impressed by Simon's work ethic and drive: "If you want to make a lot of money in property you need to treat it like a business. Simon has certainly taken it on properly. He had a job and then was at university learning about business at the weekend. Now, with his training from the academy, he is a property entrepreneur making very good money, and also has a job working long hours. He is clearly a driven person which is essential for success in this industry."

SIMON'S TIPS

"If you want to go into property do your research and get some training."

"Choose your strategy and just go for it."

"You need to put in hard work to succeed."

Chapter 13 – Ben Rumer

Property millionaire who joined academy doubles his income

Members of Samuel Leeds' academy have varying degrees of experience in property when they arrive on their first training module with notebooks in hand. Some are beginners who enrolled straight after attending the *Property Investors Crash Course*. Others, like Ben Rumer, have already invested in the housing market but want to learn how to increase their profits.

In Ben's case he was a property millionaire when he signed up for the advanced training. It was a wise move. Six months after becoming a member he had more than doubled his rental income from a clutch of buy-to-lets by implementing creative strategies designed to boost his takings.

His earnings shot up from around £2,000 to £5,000 a month and his portfolio doubled in size, rising in value to £2.2m, although that figure fluctuates.

"Obviously that goes up and down with flips and developments. You're selling properties all the time and taking on new properties. So, it does vary," he explains.

With the knowledge he gained on the training Ben added some serviced accommodation units to his bundle which means his income also varies, depending on the time of year.

"In the winter we're making between £4,000 and £5,000. In the summer it's usually much more with the tourists."

Ben, who is from Portsmouth, was introduced to Property Investors' multi-millionaire founder Samuel Leeds when he saw him in the BBC documentary, *The Week the Landlords Moved In*. The programme challenged successful landlords to live in one of their own rentals on their tenant's budget to show them what it would be like.

A few years later, when Ben had already started investing in property, he discovered Samuel's training company. At the time he had a good salary as an architect. His partner was also earning well and between them they had four buy-to-lets.

As Ben describes it, they were 'living the life.'

"We bought a Range Rover and had a nice house, but I was working eight hours at least every day. It was not the life I wanted. I have a very entrepreneurial mindset and I really wanted to build something for myself – a legacy. And I just let myself become too comfortable. I stayed in that job far too long.

"When I came across Samuel's training it pushed me to explore other ways to increase my passive income and really achieve my dream."

The Covid pandemic brought about the change Ben had been seeking. In the summer of 2020, he was made redundant. Having already participated in an online *Property Investors Crash Course,* he set up his own company instead of trying to find another job.

His first step was to purchase a buy, refurbish, refinance project. On reflection, he says it was a 'slow burner' in terms of bringing in money quickly. His efforts should have been focused on upping his passive income from his rents to replace his wage.

Despite this, he says he was still able to pull out all his money which he had invested in his BRR venture, giving him a free a house effectively, in addition to a rental profit of about £600 a month.

"The crash course and joining the academy, those first nuggets of training pushed me to raise the standard on that house and get all of the money back out."

It also taught him how important it is to implement strategies which generate a quick injection of cash if you have no reserves to fall back on or find yourself in a situation like Ben was in.

"That's what the academy has taught me, the need for a fast pound. Before I was a typical, slow buy-to-let investor. I'd buy a property, save and remortgage the deposits.

"Coming into the academy and learning from Samuel, I realised you can actually use other strategies, such as serviced accommodation, deal selling and HMOs, to really push your cashflow to the next level."

One of the initial changes Ben made was to turn one of his traditional buy-to-lets into a serviced accommodation house, which more than tripled his income.

"It's a mews house. We redecorated and refurbished it. As a buy to let, it was earning £800 a month and in the summer months it was just shy of £3,000. It does vary seasonally but it's still doing better than a buy-to-let."

A spurt of activity followed which saw him buy another house. This property is currently being renovated, with the investment from his initial BRR scheme. He also sold his first deal – another buy, refurbish, refinance opportunity which he found through a letting agent he uses. Ben sold it as an off-market deal through another estate agent/deal sourcer.

"That's about to go through now. The finder's fee is about £3,000. I'm splitting it with the co-sourcer because at the time I wasn't registered and couldn't sell it myself. That's a profit of £1,500 for me which is great. It's a salary for some people.

"I was looking out for properties anyway. If this investor didn't buy it, I would have bought it myself. It's a lovely house."

His target moving forward is to make money from refurbishments, drawing on his skills as a trained architect.

"I'm qualified in design, so my speciality is turning houses for quite a low cost into something really special."

Ben raised investor finance from another academy member and two of his friends, a couple, who trusted him to put some of their savings into a 'house flip' in Portsmouth. He also took out a bridging loan to help fund the purchase of the property for £175,000.

The return on investment promises to be huge, he says.

"It cost about £6,000 to refurbish, so not a lot of money, and it's just agreed a sale subject to contract, off market at £240,000.'

With the bridging fees, which are quite high, and the estate agent's selling commission, he estimates the pre-tax profit will be about £45,000 for seven weeks' work (eight weeks from completion to sale).

Ben says he found the deal through the letting agent he knows who also has a sourcing business and has lots of contacts in the area.

"I work with him quite regularly. We sold a deal together. We help each other out. He found this deal for me. I paid him a sourcing fee but I'm making a fantastic profit on it."

Having the support of other Property Investors Academy members has been a crucial part of Ben's success.

"Seeing other people's successes has wanted me to push myself and also meeting joint venture partners and being inspired to raise finance is beyond valuable. I think network is everything. As Samuel says, your network is your net worth."

The fact he is also an architect by profession has helped him enormously. Before being laid off, he was working in Chichester. He was also a commercial architect for several years in London.

"Part of my journey was working in London in the week and then every weekend driving down to Portsmouth refurbishing buy-to-let properties to try and build my portfolio. I had quite a few years of working very hard."

Ben bought his first house in 2011 and then went back to university to study for his master's degree and professional qualifications, working for a few years before he bought his first buy-to-let. He does a lot of the work on his projects himself, having become adept at decorating and DIY over the years.

"Part of my next challenge is letting go of that and outsourcing some of the work so I can grow my business to the next level.

"My background is so helpful with that. Designing properties to a really high standard and just choosing materials, colours and layouts and knowing how to get that right really benefited me," he adds.

Samuel's energy and passion for property drew Ben to his training. Unlike other training events he attended, he says he has never felt bored.

'The Property Investors training is full of energy and the networking is brilliant. I just really enjoy it. The whole atmosphere just pushes you to the next level. The network and friends I've made helps you to grow and you hold each other accountable. I've attended several more crash courses as well as the academy."

His goal by the end of 2022 is to be a cash millionaire through investing in high-end HMOs with en suites and possibly investing in Thailand, starting off with villas and building up an overseas portfolio. His partner is British-Thai and they have a nephew there and are funding his school education.

That is one reason for wanting to do well in property. Ben also admits he was a bit money-orientated at first, but his priorities have changed. Recently his grandmother was diagnosed with dementia and he wants to be able to pay for her to have the best care possible in a home.

"This is an amazing woman who's looked after me as a child and taken care of me my whole life, with my parents as well. She deserves the best and I would like to be in a position where I can fund her to have the best possible care available because I think she deserves it.

"Homes cost a minimum of about £1,000 a week. It's a huge amount of money for most people. So, realistically within the next year or so it's something I'd love to be able to help out with."

Another driving factor is to be able to do something for charity.

"I'm very passionate about equal rights. I'd like to provide houses for refugees – people coming from countries where they don't have the same rights as we do. That would be something I'd love to do in future."

Samuel says: "Ben is now full-time in property and financially fee. He's doubled his portfolio, which consists of eight properties and one corporate let, and done no-money-down deals. He's done incredibly well.

"Money gives you choices in life. It's not just about buying material things. It brings freedom and means you can do things like provide your grandma with the best care and look after your family and support charities.

"For me it's a real honour and fulfilling to be able to help people like Ben make more money, because they've got big hearts and want to benefit others."

BEN'S TIPS

"To my 10-years-younger self I'd say put education first. I learnt so much from the training that I didn't know before."

"I took out equity and bought a buy-to-let, thinking it would make me a millionaire overnight. There are so many other ways you can get into property. You don't need a huge amount of money. I've just taken on a corporate let as an SA near Portsmouth harbour. The cost of the studio is £650 a month and someone is taking it for the whole of January, which is a slow month, for £1,200. In the summer I expect to make a profit of £1,500 to £2,000 a month. You would probably need three buy-to-lets to make that."

"Having a job and a mortgage is still a good way of getting into property. When I bought my first house on the edge of London it had been empty for six years. It needed refurbishment but because of that we were able to build equity and release that to put into property. If you want to live in the best area in a house which doesn't need any work, you're not necessarily going to make any money. You need to be willing to work hard and compromise."

"If you've got a contact with someone, use it. I got my corporate let through the letting agent I know who helped me arrange that property with the landlord."

"Don't be scared. Just dive in. You don't achieve anything without taking action. I know people who have said I want to get through all the training first then I'll invest, or I just want to learn a bit more. You can take action now. I've made mistakes in the past. I've gone too slowly. I think I should have pushed myself harder in some ways."

Chapter 14 – Naomi Bui

Property Investors Academy student earns £30,000 in two months from selling deals

Businesswoman Naomi Bui is a big thinker in the opinion of her mentor, Samuel Leeds. Judging by her property dealings, she has certainly juggled some big numbers. Just two months after joining the Property Investors Academy Naomi made around £30,000 from selling deals – including £15,000 from one transaction alone. It paid for her training and even left her with some money over.

Naomi, who runs an estate agency in London and several other successful businesses, is also involved in a joint venture, with a predicted pay-off of £1.4m. In addition to this she has another money-spinning project lined up in Brighton.

She comes from a family of entrepreneurs. Her parents run a property business in Vietnam where she was born, and her grandparents were in the same field. She followed in their footsteps, starting out at 18 by renting out other people's properties in Singapore to cover her rent and university fees.

By the time Naomi eventually left Singapore to live with her husband in the

UK in 2011, she had built up a portfolio of 30 rent-to-rents which she generously passed over to a friend.

Beginning afresh, she again used the strategy to earn some money while studying for a master's degree in entrepreneurship. She took on two rent-to-rents, which gave her a valuable insight into the housing market in this country. Later she relinquished them to concentrate on her studies.

"My husband said study and focus on one thing, so I finished my master's and I started with other businesses to earn money and then put it in property,' explains Naomi. Early on, she saw this would give her the dual benefits of a passive income and capital appreciation.

The mother-of-one bought her first property with a mortgage for £385,000, recognising this made more sense than renting where they lived, although her husband was initially against the idea of taking out a loan. She also acquired a franchise in an estate agency business called RE/MAX and started helping to find houses for parents of overseas students in Britain.

"I got a lot of parents of students from Vietnam, Thailand, Hong Kong and Dubai, wanting to buy houses," recalls Naomi.

Then, as the business prospered, she began attracting investors who wanted her help to buy below market value properties in good locations which would give them a steady cashflow. So far, she has helped around 1,000 people to purchase a house in London. She aims to knock at least 20 per cent off the asking price through her negotiations.

She has now sold the franchise in India, the Philippines, Thailand and ten provinces of Vietnam, where she aims to introduce it nationwide and eventually globally. Alongside this activity, she also operates an accountancy and restaurant/takeaway business.

It was with this wealth of commercial experience under her belt that Naomi attended a *Property Investors Crash Course* after being impressed by Samuel Leeds' popular YouTube videos.

The date of the course – September 17, 2021 – is engraved in her mind as it was her birthday.

"My father said to me, 'what do you want for your birthday.' I said I want to go to the crash course and meet Samuel Leeds."

Naomi got her wish, meeting Samuel at the crash course. They got on with each other instantly.

"It changed my life, even though I had got experience [of property]. I liked Samuel's energy and it was positive. I knew it was for me and said I want to buy the whole programme. I didn't even know it was called the academy. I wanted to get in because I think we share the same character of wanting to act on things."

She adds: "A lot of people, even my clients, said to me why go to the crash course and the academy because you've done everything before. I said everything has changed, even with buy, refurbish, refinance. I love this strategy. Not everyone knows about it."

Naomi spent £11,995 on the Property Investors Academy which provides members with an in-depth knowledge of different investment strategies through a series of training courses. They are also given mentorship, access to a *Mastermind* forum and opportunities to network.

The entrepreneur says she made her money back in the first fortnight after learning about how to source and package property deals for investors in return for a fee. The size of the deal determines her commission.

"After the first two days I sold a small deal for £2,000. Then I sold a big deal, which was actually two properties, for £15,000."

Having seen the excellent returns to be gained from investing in real estate, Naomi decided to purchase a property herself in Brighton for £790,000. The house has seven rooms with planning permission to create another two.

"I will spend about £7,000 doing it up and then run it as a serviced accommodation business. I've already got another SA there which got 95 per cent occupancy in 2021, right up to lockdown."

Her existing furnished accommodation in Brighton turns over £25,000 a month, leaving her with a profit of £8,000. She expects her new SA property will have an even higher turnover of about £28,000 per month.

Naomi plans to refinance the mortgage which will enable her to pull out money to reinvest in another project. Once the house has been improved and extended, she estimates the end value will be £950,000, out of which she will keep £140,000 after costs from just this one deal.

At the same time the entrepreneur has joined forces with a joint venture partner to undertake a commercial scheme in central London. The intention is to buy a building and add another storey to it to maximise their return on investment. She anticipates the profit on that one will be £1.4m which she will split with her partner.

As with any development, it takes time to see the money in the bank. By contrast, deal sourcing generates a 'quick pound.'

Learning how to package and sell deals, including negotiating the purchase price and setting out the financial benefits, has also helped her attract new investors.

"Now I know what exactly the strategy is and the correct formula. It's clearer for my investor and they love it."

She adds: "I always tell the investor to view the property and focus on the formula. It's never about feeling because they're not going to live there. I'm always clear and transparent with them."

Some of her investors have been doing business with her for a decade and know how she works. Her approach to sourcing deals differs from her role as an estate agent.

"I have to teach my customer how to buy the deal. I ask them what profit they want to make, where they want to buy and how much money they've got. They have to pay first and after that 100 per cent my team works for them finding a deal until they're happy with that. It's not the estate agent way where someone buys a house and then pays you."

Similarly, when she is trying to clinch a rent-to-rent deal she makes her terms clear.

"I say to the owner never think of it as you are giving me the chance. We give you the chance. I guarantee you the rent. You don't need to worry. You don't have a void period. I take care of your property. Whenever you want to come you can come. I've got my business. I'm not living there.

"After that I do my due diligence. Is it worth it or not? It has to be fair. No one works for free. And the landlord says, 'OK, I accept the offer. Here's the key.' This is a way I'm helping the landlord. It's not about them helping me. It's a win-win. We are there to manage it and they say thank you. Otherwise, they rent it to someone else, like a poor student, and don't necessarily know they're going to get the money. It's not guaranteed they can pay the rent next month."

She checks the references of prospective tenants.

Hard work and dedication have got Naomi where she is today. She frequently works into the early hours of the morning to serve her clients.

"I work till 4am if I've still got a job to do. With all my businesses I'm the only one to know from start to end what is happening with my customer. With my clients from Vietnam and other countries, I'm helping them to buy a house and settle in the UK. I follow it right through."

The Property Investors Academy has been a constant source of support to her, with coaches who have given her invaluable advice. She has also made friends who help and motivate one another.

"It's a place where we can trust each other and do business."

During her training Naomi challenged herself to secure a rent-to-rent agreement to apply what Samuel had taught her. She found it tough, receiving several rejections before she got a 'yes.'

She was successful after seeking the help of her mentor and modifying her script when talking to landlords. Afterwards she sold the deal because she didn't have time to manage it herself.

When she started out Naomi worried about her image as she was a foreigner and English was not her first language. In time, however, she came round to the view that this was no barrier.

"You can be a property investor and not born in the UK. The chance is there for everyone."

As far as Naomi is concerned, the UK is the best country in the world to invest in and London the best city, although she is now casting her net further afield.

Over the next two years she plans to focus on taking on more buy, refurbish, refinance projects as she tries to capitalise on what she has learnt so far.

"Samuel was the right person to meet at the right time. I'm looking forward to working with him and everyone else in the academy to build up my portfolio."

Samuel says: "We hit it off straight away because Naomi is a savvy lady and has got really good energy. She's a big thinker who makes a lot of money on the deals she sells. Her confidence helps and the fact she goes in with business acumen.

"All through the lockdowns she's been building and growing. It's ridiculously impressive. She's a massive asset to the academy and I'm really excited about helping her to go to a whole new level."

He adds: "I always say on the academy there are only two reasons why you can fail – one because you don't take any action and when you get stuck you don't ask for help. Naomi made sure she acted on what she'd been taught and sought advice when she needed it."

NAOMI'S TIPS

"Everything is about action. You have to think and do it. When you do it, focus and see it through to the end."

"When you meet positive, successful people, everything will come to you."

"Always be transparent and clear. Sometimes people don't like you to be direct with them, but it's always the best way. When I'm direct, slowly they love me more."

"Learn to say no sometimes. I always qualify my customers. I don't serve everyone because I don't have time for everything."

"Practice. The more you do that, the more confident you get."

"Ninety-five per cent of my customers come from referrals. That's so important because people trust you then. In the last two days, an investor referred me a customer who is moving from New York to London and wants to buy a £50m penthouse."

"With a rent-to-rent agreement, never think of it as the landlord giving you the chance. You are guaranteeing them a rent and you take care of their property. I do due diligence and ask myself if it is worth it or not. It has to be fair. No one works for free. This is the way I'm helping them. It's a win-win."

"If you're thinking of coming to a Property Investors Crash Course, just do it. There's no time for thinking. It will only cost you £1."

"The best investors invest in themselves. If you've got the money and are serious about pursuing property, join the academy. The training is brilliant. You meet people you can trust, and you can go for it together."

Chapter 15 – Aydin Guner

Property millionaire started lockdown with just £500 in the bank

In the space of 18 months, Aydin Guner went from having a home with a mortgage and a steady job to becoming a serial investor in property, using the buy, refurbish, refinance strategy. He is about to complete the purchase of his fifth house which will make him a property millionaire and that is just the start. With the help of Property Investors, he is hoping to pull off bigger deals as he flexes his entrepreneurial muscles to try out other wealth creation methods.

Everyone has their own story of how they got into property. Aydin was working from home on his own during the pandemic when, during a spare moment, his thoughts turned to doing something else with his life. As he describes it:

"I had about £500 in my bank account. It's raining outside and miserable and I'm not seeing anybody. So, I just started looking on YouTube and came across Samuel Leeds. I thought, 'Who is this guy talking about property?'

"I'd never heard of him before. I didn't know too much about property either. I just thought it was something rich folk did, and you need loads of capital to get started. But I just had something in me that wanted more."

It was that yearning for something else which led Aydin on a journey of discovery. In his words, he consumed the information Samuel was giving out in his videos about refinancing a property. Aydin found out that it was possible to release the equity on his house to obtain investment funds.

Nearly everyone Aydin spoke to about this idea warned him against doing it, including his own father.

"They said, 'Why do you want to get yourself in more debt? I love my dad. He's been really supportive, but he was one of the ones who was saying find a good bank, get a mortgage and stick with them."

His father advised him strongly not to put himself at risk by remortgaging his home, but Aydin decided he did not have much to lose. He had a job he liked, but it was not making him wealthy.

The 36-year-old read motivational business books which taught him the difference between good and bad debt, and how the rich have assets while the middle class have debt.

"It was almost like I'm an alien and all these new things are coming to me. I thought I need to start implementing these principles."

Aydin found a mortgage broker on the Wirral who suggested to him he could raise a certain amount of money from the property he was living in. Having been told he could access up to 75 per cent of the value of his house, he took out £25,000.

"I'd never had that much money in my bank before. I felt so rich. It doesn't seem like much but to me at the time this was good money."

He started looking for a house on the Wirral, which would make a good investment, but the market was so competitive that by the time he put in an offer on a property it had already been sold.

Despite this, Aydin got lucky when he managed to buy a house in the area for £80,000, putting down a deposit of £20,000 (25 per cent of the purchase price). It was at that point that his experience as a project manager came in handy.

Aydin realised his skills, working with budgets and planning, could be transferred to the property sector. Having been a salesman in the past, he was also able to negotiate hard to bring down the cost of doing up the property to less than £5,000.

"I got a really nice kitchen for around £2,000. It was from a rapid kitchens place in Liverpool and a bathroom for £2,000. I also got the electrics set up and did a lot of painting myself. For less than £5,000 I was able to boost the value of this property to £132,000."

As he puts it, he struck gold.

Aydin closely followed the principles and teachings of Property Investors' founder to give himself the best chance of success.

"I read his *Buy Low Rent High* book and binge watched hours of his videos of how to renovate a property, get a good deal, and search the market. I was such a newcomer to it."

Aydin recognises he was fortunate to secure such a good deal. Nevertheless, he was stunned by how much money he made.

"In a matter of months, I'd gone from having £500 and being miserable on my own in lockdown to having £40,000 in my bank account. So, I just carried on."

One of Aydin's recommendations for anyone aspiring to be a property investor is to assemble a power team of people who can be trusted.

"I've got a really good broker, a real estate agent and brilliant solicitors who I can call at any time. We help each other. We make things happen."

With the £40,000 picked up from refinancing the mortgage on his first investment property, Aydin bought two more in Liverpool. He repeated the process of refurbishing them and then refinancing them to unlock cash for another two acquisitions.

"It's so bizarre but I almost became desensitised to the money. It didn't feel like I was wasting £50,000. I was investing and using the principles that Samuel communicated on his videos."

The fledgling entrepreneur could not even paint a wall when he started out and was 'a terrible DIY person,' but slowly he learned how to carry out simple tasks to keep down his renovation costs.

The ability to haggle with contractors and not accept their first price also saved him money.

"I'm a salesman at heart. For 10 years of my early life, I was in sales and Samuel teaches great principles. He has a system in place of what people can do from zero to being financially free.

"There is skill involved as well. It's a bit like climbing Everest. A teacher like Samuel gives you the right equipment and shows you how to climb. Even the Sherpas drag people up the mountain, but there are going to be times when they have to jump over a wall themselves. That's where your natural skill comes in."

That was demonstrated when Aydin managed to persuade one owner to sell her property to him, even though she had already accepted a higher offer. His tactic was to message her through the Purplebricks estate agency. Introducing himself as a young investor who lived ten minutes away and loved her house, he suggested they meet up to discuss a deal.

After establishing a rapport with her, she accepted his offer, which was £6,000 less than the initial offer of £112,000.

"I thought to myself I've actually sold something there. She's left £6,000 on the table to work with me. So, you need to have good people skills and work on building a rapport. I thought that was really profound."

One childhood memory which left a lasting impression on Aydin was a conversation he had with his father.

"I remember we were watching a boxing match on TV with Chris Eubank and I said, 'dad I'd love to go to Vegas one day to see a fight' and he said, 'no people like us don't go to events like that.'

"I thought to myself what does he mean by people like us? Then I've heard people say if you go to Dubai or Miami, it's fake. People like us don't go to places like that. That's a different world.

"That's always stuck with me because it's like why is it fake? Why can't you enjoy the nicer things? It's like some people are living in this matrix. Anything outlandish and cool is just not attainable and it isn't for you.

"What I was getting from certain people was almost like be quiet, sit in the corner and do your job and that's it. Do what everyone else does. For me it was, actually I don't want to do what everybody else is doing. I don't want to be in a job all my life not thriving.

"Breaking away from that was like stepping out of the matrix. It was very difficult and all the while I'm battling with these emotions and thoughts: no, no, don't do it."

It was watching Samuel's free YouTube videos which encouraged Aydin to take the plunge into property investing. As in any field, there are risks. In property, the market could crash or there could be a damp problem, for example, which costs thousands of pounds to fix. As a project manager this is something he is used to dealing with, but believes good planning mitigates risks.

"There are always going to be problems, but you have to try and plan ahead for that and mitigate those problems. Nothing ever goes smoothly. It's just how you plan the project that matters."

He adds: "Taking action is really important. It took a long time and a lot of tunnel vision to take that first step of refinancing my existing place.

"Now it doesn't feel like a big step. I'd do it ten times over but at the time it was, 'Is this safe. Is this right? Everyone else is saying don't do it. I can't be the only one that feels that way.' Taking action and planning for problems is the key."

Aydin's reason for going into property is to give himself the freedom to pursue his own ventures.

"I work with great people and enjoy what I do. I'm not in a position where I want to leave my day job, but I don't want to do that for the rest of my life.

"My goal in life is just to have a bit more freedom to work on my own projects. Obviously, there are also financial goals that I've set myself.

"We have a sort of depression pandemic in the world where a lot of people are miserable. It's because they don't have any goals. They're not working to anything. They're just in a job they trudge along to.

"I'm very goal driven. I'm happiest when I'm collaborating with other people, working on big deals.

"The last 18 months have been really fun as well. I've had more fun in the last two years than ever really. I've been able to go on a nice holiday in Dubai and stay in a villa with my girlfriend. I could never have done that before.

"I don't think money gives you happiness, but it opens doors and gives you that freedom. I just want more and more now. It's like a drug almost, that feeling of success, and I just want the deals to get bigger and bigger."

His mentor Samuel is impressed by Aydin's achievements so far. He says: "Aydin completed the perfect buy, refurbish, refinance deal with his first deal and now he's about to become a property millionaire and move on to other strategies like rent-to-rent and HMOs with the help of our courses. He's also about to buy another house for £200,000. I can't wait to see him becoming a property multi-millionaire.

"With a BRR there are three figures you need to get right: making sure you buy at the right price, the refurb comes in at the right price and the end value is high enough for you to refinance and pull your money out with 75 per cent loan to value."

AYDIN'S TIPS

"If you want to refurbish a house cheaply, remove the wallpaper, sand it all down and give it two or three coats of white paint. I also use Polyfilla to cover any gaps."

"You can buy cheap light fixtures for £15 to £20 that look nice. I paid an electrician £200 for a couple of days to put them in."

"Haggle with contractors. Don't take their first price."

"There are going to be ups and downs. Fortune favours the brave and you have to persevere."

"If you've got a goal, go for it. Don't listen to negativity."

"It's been said before, but if your goals don't scare you a little bit then they're not high enough.

"Be ambitious and surround yourself with good people."

Chapter 16 – Arnaldo Pierre

Former Army man marches to success with two free houses and land in the Caribbean

Even if you do not have thousands of pounds sitting in the bank, you have to find ways to tap into money if you want to be successful in property. This principle is at the core of what Samuel Leeds teaches his students – to be resourceful and find solutions.

Arnaldo Pierre, who is a member of the Property Investors Academy, took this lesson to heart when he embarked on his property journey and is reaping the rewards already. Arnaldo financed his first buy, refurbish, refinance project by taking out a loan against the value of his house and using some savings.

That deal then enabled him to pull out all his money to buy a second investment house. This time he even made a profit after renovating the property and remortgaging it. He also derives a passive income from renting out his two houses and is now set to become a property developer.

With his gains, Arnaldo bought some land in Saint Vincent, where he was born, to provide luxury apartments for tourists and is also benefiting from a separate rent-to-rent arrangement.

All of this was achieved in just seven months of being on the academy. Arnaldo, who is an enthusiastic advocate of Samuel Leeds and his training company, says it's been an amazing ride.

"Anyone who hasn't been on a Samuel Leeds course needs to get down there. You walk through the door, and you leave as a machine. You leave with the confidence where you can just walk into any estate agency."

Arnaldo was raised on the Caribbean island of Saint Vincent, moving to the UK in 2008, where he served in the British Army until 2012 before leaving to take up an IT career. He later became interested in property which is something he pursues alongside his job.

The deal that set him on the path to wealth came after he attended Property investors' *Buy, Refurbish, Refinance* course. He went along to an auction and snapped up a house in Durham for £47,000. Compared to property prices where he lives in High Wycombe, it seemed to him like the cheapest house purchase ever.

After spending £19,000 on a full refurbishment, it was revalued at £90,000. By remortgaging the property to its new value, Arnaldo was able to recoup all of his money, effectively giving him a free house.

"A refinance is actually easy if you're taught how to do it. You get a mortgage after you've done the work. You uplift the value, then you pull your money back out once you get the new value," he explains.

Arnaldo had to comb the market to find the house but once he had viewed it, he knew it would work as an investment.

"I knew the figures were going to work out and then I put my offer in. I completed on it within 28 days. That's the advantage of auctions. The process is fast.

"In the training courses you are taught not to wait until you complete to start getting builders to give you quotes. I arranged that with the estate agents so that by the time the exchange on the property was completed it was time for the builders to go in.

"This is the importance of having training because when you've got the knowledge and the support, you're able to do things more smoothly."

Managing the house from a distance proved no problem. He found a letting agent after asking Samuel's wife Amanda for a recommendation. As Samuel and Amanda have properties in Durham themselves, she was able to refer him to their agent.

"I was hungry at this point," Arnaldo recalls. "I couldn't sleep at night. I was going to sleep in the early hours of the morning, looking for my next opportunity and still learning."

He again managed to grab a bargain at auction, buying a house in Maidenhead, which was nearer to his home, for £155,000. Using builders who do work on his own property, he refurbished it for £12,000.

This time the returns were spectacular by anyone's standards.

"The refinance valuation came back at £240,000. I was on a training course when my mortgage broker messaged me saying £180,000 is going to be hitting your bank. It was an amazing feeling to pull out all my money and some more.

"That's being rented out as a single let at the moment. We've been taught to use different strategies but that one is bringing me £1,150 a month, so I thought I'm just going to leave it as it is."

Arnaldo is looking forward to tackling his next venture which is to build four luxury apartments on his land in Saint Vincent. They will be furnished and rented out to holidaymakers, giving him yet more income to put into further investment schemes.

His mentor, Samuel, will be the first guest on his invitation list, Arnaldo promises.

There are many advantages with serviced accommodation that a single let lacks, he points out, especially as his coach drums into his students that cashflow is king.

'When you're looking at serviced accommodation it's almost like you're looking at a rental on steroids. If I want to get a guest out, I can get them out straight away. When you've got a single let you've got less money coming in. Also, if you need your property back there's a process. We know how hard it is these days to get a tenant out, whereas SA is creative, it is exciting, and you get a lot of cashflow out of it."

His training has taught him the tax benefits to be had with SAs as well. There are capital allowances with furnished holiday lets which is why in future he will be focusing on that as a strategy.

"Going forward most of my properties are going to be, SAs."

When asked what his hardest moment has been so far in his journey, Arnaldo struggles to come up with an answer. He says this is because he was able to follow the training programme step-by-step which made it easy to execute.

His education in property helped him to secure his rent-to-rent agreement, even when faced with reluctance from one agent to do business with him. Arnaldo and another academy member decided to walk into an estate agency, just as Samuel does on his *Financial Freedom Challenges,* to try to pin down a deal.

It was Christmas and there were only two letting agencies open. The first agent told them they no longer arranged company lets after having an issue with one. Arnaldo was ready with a response.

"Straight away I said we have invested and gone to the Property Investors Academy and learned all we need to learn to be able to execute this correctly. We've got lots of other properties and we're doing it successfully.

"He took my details and said if it's something we're going to look into again we'll contact you. In our training we always get told go for no's with the expectation of getting a yes. You're going to get knock-backs and no's but don't let it demotivate you. It was important to be there and experience that first-hand. So, it didn't really knock us back.

"We had one more letting agency to walk into and so we did. We explained what we were looking for and what we were going to be doing and the agent offered us a two-bedroom house.

"I said if you can give us the address, we can have a look at the details. We'll let you know if we think it works. I went home and had a look at it. It was literally right next to the hospital in Maidenhead and there was another SA on the same road. So, I had a good example to analyse what that SA was doing."

Arnaldo saw that it was performing well and so emailed the agent on the spot to say he would love to view the house if the owner was open to the idea of renting it to them as a company let.

"Because this letting agent was accustomed to doing these types of deal and the landlord had trust in the agent it was a bit easier to convince her that this could be a potential long-term let for her."

The network support engineer was on a Property Investors training event when he got a call to say the landlady was 'in.'

"I thought I'm going right now. I looked around it and there was not much to do to it. I said we don't need to wait until the morning. We'll have it."

After tying up the arrangement, he returned to his course so full of excitement that he had to share his good news with his trainer-in-chief

Samuel.

"It's been absolutely amazing being on the academy and having someone to come back to and tell them what you've done – and to be able to speak to a real person if you've got any questions or issues.

"Just seeing Samuel and being supported is heart-warming. That gave me even more confidence to go on and do it again and again."

Arnaldo is now waiting to complete on the contracts.

Looking ahead, Arnaldo is planning to venture into deal sourcing and concentrate on adding more properties to his portfolio. He also wants to 'give back' by attending Property Investors' crash courses to talk about his experience in property. Another ambition is to help the wider community.

He was rushed into that process when La Soufriere volcano on Saint Vincent erupted in April 2021, resulting in about 15 per cent of the population having to move into temporary accommodation. He set up a charity to support people affected by the disaster and sent four 40ft containers with supplies to the island.

He has already begun speaking to would-be investors at free Property Investors events while at the same time balancing his work commitments with his dealings in the housing market.

"I explain how I got to where I am and advise them you need to get educated. There's no point trying to come to the free ones only. Once you come on this training, there's no going back."

His wife has supported him in his property activities, accompanying him to a few viewings and Property Investors courses including free ones.

"She needs to experience that energy Samuel brings and then she can understand why I'm coming home so fired up after viewing properties and not sleeping at night!"

Samuel praises Arnaldo for how quickly and effectively he has implemented what he has been taught. He says: "Most people spend their whole life wanting to get on the property ladder, buying one house or maybe two. Arnaldo is buying houses super-fast and has worked hard. He's a smart guy and an action taker. Combine that with support and training and you've got the ingredients for becoming a property millionaire. He deserves his success.

"I love training people like Arnaldo because he's got a massive heart. He's already set a charity up and he is giving back. That's what I want my students to aspire to – to be compassionate capitalists."

ARNALDO'S TIPS

"Get educated. if you don't have the education and you're just having a bash at property it could be one of the most expensive bashes you have. It's like any other trade you need to get that education before you go on further."

"It's easy to be successful when you're around people who are successful, like in the academy and at the Christmas party where everybody was in their element doing deals. If you're just sitting at home watching YouTube videos and getting rejected, it's harder to succeed."

"Coming from my background, it's not been easy. There have been times in the past where people are looking at you differently because you are succeeding. You're going to get that on your way up which is why it's even more important to surround yourself with people who've got common interests and goals."

Samuel Leeds

Chapter 17 – Jay Twiss

Musician is on song with rent-to-rents and making £12k profit per month

When rap artist Jay Twiss is not performing, he spends his free time pursuing his other passion for property investing.

Jay, who has been mentored by Samuel Leeds, has become a prolific player in the market, having built up a rent-to-rent portfolio of 44 rooms which produce a revenue of around £25,000 a month. He pays the landlords an agreed monthly rent and in return is allowed to let out the accommodation at a higher rate. The difference between the two amounts is his margin. After deducting any maintenance costs, for which he is responsible, Jay is left with a profit of £12,000 a month.

It has made him financially independent, quite apart from what he earns as a musician. However, his path to wealth was not without its challenges. He had to shrug off a year of refusals before sealing his first deal.

In fact, Jay admitted defeat after spending the whole of 2019 attempting to tie up an investment without success. That changed when he watched one of Samuel's *Financial Freedom Challenges* on YouTube and was filled with renewed enthusiasm to try his hand at being a property entrepreneur.

The singer attended a free *Property Investors Crash Course* which taught him the basics of assessing a deal and calculating the return on investment.

"I learnt a lot there. Samuel gave us quite a few spreadsheets as well which was useful," Jay recalls.

Equipped with this information, he viewed properties in his home city of Sheffield with the objective of sourcing deals for investors and picking up commissions for himself. It was here that Samuel had proved it was possible to become financially free in a week with no money to start off with.

"When I saw that video on YouTube, it pumped me up again. I thought, 'That's incredible. This is not real. I have to try it myself.' I did and it's worked out."

Jay managed to make money from deal selling which he then ploughed into investing in his own deals.

Deciding to widen his search, he found a property in Huddersfield which he thought was 'perfect' for a rent-to-rent. Unfortunately for Jay, the landlord was unfamiliar with the business model. Undeterred, Jay went on the hunt for another opening through the estate agent he had just dealt with.

"I thought this estate agent is willing to work with me on a rent-to-rent basis. So, I went and looked on the estate agent's website for other properties which potentially could be good rent-to-rents."

His tactic paid off. All 44 of his rent-to-rent units were obtained through this estate agent and two others he contacted.

Jay says the best agents to approach are the ones who understand the concept.

"You get some estate agents who have worked with other people doing this and don't like it, or they've worked with someone who has done this and they're willing to take on more people like you. You also find estate agents who don't know what rent-to-rent is."

Jay draws up a list of all the estate agents in the area he is targeting, and then calls them until he finds one who has already had experience of arranging a rent-to-rent agreement.

"In every city there will be an estate agent who knows about rent-to-rents so you will eventually find one."

Making a list enables him to quickly locate an estate agent who can help him negotiate an agreement. He prefers to deal with a real estate professional, rather than the landlord directly.

"Some landlords go with their emotions, and you have to try to convince them if they don't know the model. They take it personally: "do I really want to let this guy in? When actually I'm a company and I want the property on a business lease for five or ten years."

Before clinching his all-important first deal, he had agreed another one, only for the owner to withdraw when he learnt that an investor would be taking it on and not Jay.

"As soon as I introduced the investor, I got a reply from the estate agent that the landlord didn't want to carry on with it. Maybe the landlord wondered why someone else was coming on board."

Jay suffered many rejections before coming to the crash course and then enrolling on the *Deal Selling Masterclass*. He was impressed with both the quality of the training he received, and the way his mentor Samuel delivered it.

"He's amazing and easy to work with. At the *Deal Selling Masterclass* he told everyone what they needed to do and gave them a task. I also noticed that he gave you all the information but didn't just let it go there. He told us if we needed any help, we could reach out to him or one of his coaches, so if we didn't reach out that was our fault.

"Samuel does give further help after the training, so I don't see how anyone could go wrong unless they're lazy and they're just not putting in the work."

Although Jay has now been investing in property for a few years, also offering serviced accommodation in Manchester, he still seeks Samuel's advice.

"I contacted him a couple of days ago about a contract. I agree with him that no man is an island. You need to get around good people."

Jay's healthy income from his portfolio has enabled him to employ his sister full-time in the business to give him time for his other activities. He is a busy man. As well as continuing his musical career, he has a full-time job as a design engineer.

In December 2021, he released *Gold Diggers*, a hip-hop/rap single inspired by his experience of life since becoming successful.

"Everyone wants a piece. They see you do well and expect you to pay for everything. That's fine if we were grafted together and you're struggling. I'm happy to help you. But if I don't know you, then show me you're not just here because I'm living a good lifestyle. Once we become friends then maybe I can help you."

Having developed 'the mindset of an investor,' Jay is eager to expand his business as more opportunities come his way and he carries on trying to dig out gold for himself with help from Property Investors' trainers.

Samuel says being in the right environment with experts and like-minded people on hand to provide advice and support opens so many doors for newcomers to the property industry.

"If you work hard and when you get stuck you ask for help, and ask the right people, you kind of can't fail. The reason Jay probably struggled so much in the first year was because he wasn't asking for help. He didn't have anyone he could go to for advice. You can only learn so much on YouTube. Having a mentor guiding you and a good support network behind you are crucial.

"Jay's rent-to-rent business is now turning over £25,000 to £30,000 per month which is incredible. Despite 12 months of struggle and rejection, in the end it took just three people to say yes to him. That's important for anyone trying to become a property investor to remember. You're three yeses away from becoming financially free like Jay who is making a profit of £12,000 a month.

"He deserves congratulations for everything he has achieved in property and in music. I'm looking forward to helping him take his business to a whole new level."

JAY'S TIPS

"It's very important to have people you can rely on."

"I use SpareRoom to find out what the demand for accommodation is like in a particular area. I do this before I sign an agreement with a landlord."

"Work hard and make sure you get training. I should have done that sooner."

"Find estate agents with knowledge of rent-to-rents in your target area and make a list which you can also draw on in future."

Chapter 18 – Rebecca Murray

Academy student built £2m portfolio in two years with business partner

In two years, Rebecca Murray has gone from knowing absolutely nothing about property to becoming the director of a company making an average profit of £11,000 a month from a £2m real estate portfolio. Rebecca has also secured a lease option agreement on a land deal with a Gross Development Value of £9m which promises to make her even more money.

What also makes Rebecca's story so impressive is the fact she started out with just £2,000 to invest after watching Samuel Leeds' videos and joining the Property Investors Academy.

Right from the beginning she was determined to try her hand at every strategy taught in the academy to achieve success.

"I wanted to open my options up. So that's why I went into the academy, looked at every strategy and just tried everything," says Rebecca.

Hard work and dedication have contributed to her meteoric progress. Rebecca has watched so many of Samuel's YouTube videos that even her young daughter recognises his face, she says, while her husband jokes that it feels like he has moved in with them because he is always on the 'telly.'

She admits it has become something of an obsession.

"I watched one video, then that was it. I couldn't stop watching them. I've still got a folder at home from when I started. It's really thick and it's packed with everything I've written off Samuel's YouTube channel. I just got addicted to that and then I was like, that's it we're going to the crash course. From there came the academy and I've just gone upwards since."

Rebecca still studies the videos now from time to time to remind herself of anything she may have forgotten. She acknowledges that she would not be where she is today without the help of Property Investors' multi-millionaire founder and his team.

"I can't thank them enough. I would never have achieved what I have done without the Property Investors Academy and the people I've had around me.

Rebecca was searching for another enterprise to pursue alongside her signs and graphics business when she discovered Samuel's YouTube channel and then read his books. However, it was only during one of the lockdowns, after joining the academy, that she set her mind on becoming a property entrepreneur.

"In lockdown, when Samuel did all the nightly calls to keep everyone motivated, that's when I really felt I had this passion for it. If I feel something so strongly, I know I'm going to go for it."

Her first move was to team up with another Property Investors Academy member, David Taylor. Together they formed a company called Rave Investments – a combination of their two names – which was incorporated in December 2020.

"When we started Rave Investments, that was when I realised there was no going back for me," recalls Rebecca.

They began modestly by acquiring a buy-to-let.

"It was mid-Covid when everything was shut down. We found this deal and decided to keep it because it was a good little buy-to-let. The purchase price was £50,000, but it took that long to go through – about 12 months – that it was worth £60,000 by the time we purchased it.

"We sold a deal in the meantime and project managed it as well. So that paid for the deposit. It was a free house to us."

An investor in London bought the deal after they offered it to a list of potential customers generated from their contacts and reaching out on social media sites, including Samuel Leeds' platforms.

From day one, Rebecca's ambition was to scale up and become a property millionaire, although it has been difficult balancing all their separate commitments.

"We've been working day and night with having our own businesses alongside. It's not been an easy road at all, but we've just been carrying on. We've just been very active with every opportunity that's come to us, or we've found.

"Networking across Samuel Leeds' platforms and all social media and going to the events – it's all been amassed through that," explains Rebecca.

At times she pinches herself because she cannot believe how quickly they have grown and how much they have accumulated since Rave Investments was set up just over a year ago.

"I'm still in a whirlwind of making things happen. I don't even sit down to look at the figures. I'm just on to the next one and the next one...Then when we finally sit down, we say have we really done this?"

She is used to putting in the hours.

"My husband says to me, 'If there's anyone who can do it, you can do it.' He doesn't know anyone who works as hard as me, so if I want something I'll go and get it."

In the early days, other members of her family had no idea she was involved in property because she kept a low profile.

"I didn't tell anybody at first. I kept it quiet. Then as time has gone on, and I've grown more, people have got to know, and they've been really supportive. It got to a point where I couldn't hide any more what I was doing. It was all over social media and people were seeing me in different areas asking me questions. Even in the signs business, people started asking me about it.

"I realised a lot of my customers were in property, so we had something else to talk about as well. It all tied in nicely."

In hindsight, Rebecca realises her initial reluctance to be open was motivated by a desire to show people what she had done, instead of telling them what she was going to do.

Certainly, her property deals speak for her these days. They include two rent-to-rents and four HMOs. One of the rent-to-rents is a two-bedroom apartment in Manchester city centre. Rebecca and her business partner David plan to turn the other one in Liverpool into a 'party pad.'

Many people providing furnished accommodation for short stays, as they are, prohibit parties. Theirs, however, will be specifically designed for this purpose. Each of the three floors in the apartment will sleep eight people, with the top floor separated off for couples only.

"We found when we did our research that there are all these party pads but where are couples going to go? They can go to a Premier Inn, but it would be nice to have somewhere right in the centre, next to all the bars, where they can go and enjoy themselves," says Rebecca.

The four HMOs have been financed by joint ventures found through the Property Investors Academy, as well as investors asking to work with them.

"People see we're active and have got experience, and they like us as people. They trust us," she adds.

Two of the properties are next door to each other in Burnley. The plan is to turn each one into a six-bedroom house share and convert the basements into two-bed apartments. These flats may be sold off to fund other projects.

Rebecca says she and David, a structural engineer, work well as a team, bouncing ideas off each other and covering for one another. If something needs doing on the property side and David is busy with his consultancy business, Rebecca will take over, and vice versa.

This collaboration even extended to David driving Rebecca to Samuel Leeds' house to be interviewed for his YouTube *Winners on a Wednesday* show because she was occupied completing a deal.

"I was on my laptop as usual and made £3,999 from selling the deal," Rebecca reveals.

David has also appeared on *Winners on a Wednesday* to talk about his success. They are both single-minded when it comes to tackling jobs. Their priority is to tie up the deal first, and then obtain builders' quotes for any renovation work required before finding someone to fund the project.

Not everyone would have the courage to adopt this bold approach, but years of being in business have given Rebecca the confidence to press on, even when there is no partner waiting in the wings.

"You can't worry about those things, or you'll never get there. If it's a good deal and the deal stacks, it's going to go. It's a no brainer to me."

Rebecca says what distinguishes a successful entrepreneur from an employee is having that bravery to deal with the 'a, b, c' and then worry about the 'x, y, z' later.

"People who work for someone else are afraid of not succeeding, and they're afraid of the x, y, z problems. They see the negativity before they see anything else, and I think that scares a lot of people away. But you can overcome anything if you want to, or I believe I can."

Moving forward, the businesswoman has her sights set on bigger projects, although she still has her eye on refinancing the small, buy-to-let, which got her started in property investing and is now worth £70,000. Remortgaging the property to its new value will raise more cash for investing.

In the meantime, she has just agreed a lease option on a land deal which came about through her doing some networking for her signs business. It put her in touch with a builder who she later asked to give her a quote for some work on a small HMO scheme she was pricing up.

During their meeting he mentioned some other projects he was involved with. When she enquired what they were, he put her in contact with a land agent.

"This is where this joint venture deal has come from. We've got a two-year option on it, subject to planning. It's to build nine units plus a conversion. Each unit will be worth £1m. There's a planning gain of £1.1m on it, so it's massive. This is like a real learning curve for me.

"To think that it started just with a little conversation on my signs side is brilliant."

Rebecca enjoys working with others on joint ventures, describing it as a 'great experience all round.'

"There's a saying if you want to go fast, go alone but if you want to go far go together. I definitely agree with that. That's why we decided to do it like that. There are many people out there who don't want to joint venture, but we felt our personalities suited that strategy.

"We meet up with our JV partners all the time. We have breakfast and go through business matters. Even that brings future investments. We've had a couple of our JV partners now asking us to do another one. So just from that it can roll onto other things."

Her reason for being in property is simple.

"Everyone loves the money, but I love what I do. I love learning about new things all the time. I'm probably 10 per cent into my journey. I've got so much more to learn. Every bit of what I do learn I'm like, right what's the next step. I just want to progress in property and inspire my kids."

Samuel says: "Rebecca is clearly addicted to success and winning in property. To get the kind of results which she's achieved you need to not only work smart but work really hard. She has spent hours and hours out in the rain, knocking on doors to get deals. Part of her success is that she's also had good people around her. She is a very good example of somebody who knows the power of joint venturing.

"I honestly think she's the first person to come on *Winners on a Wednesday* who has not just implemented every single strategy in property but dominated in each one."

REBECCA'S TIPS

"Everything follows from putting your money into education. If I hadn't joined the Property Investors Academy, I wouldn't have met David and had my investments."

"If you're looking for a joint venture partner, first and foremost get the deal and package it up. Then you can present something good to them. Once they see the figures, at the end of the day that's what they're after. They want to see their money is going to be put to good use."

"I've learnt so much along the way from throwing myself into it. Whatever job you're going into, most of the time you won't know all the ins and outs at first."

"You've got to be in debt to make something. That's good debt. I wasn't in debt at the start but if you've got no debt and no cashflow, then you have to take a job."

Chapter 19 – Ibby and Huslen Rahman

Rent-to-serviced accommodation model enhances couple's life and bank balance

Life for Huslen Rahman was not all about being a stay-at-home mum. She felt trapped and wanted to earn some money for her family, rather than relying on her husband to make her wealthy. Property proved to be the route which would enable her to do that, lifting her out of a trough of despondency.

When the opportunity came along to get some free training, the mother-of-two grabbed it with both hands. Huslen insisted she and her husband Ibby go to a *Property Investors Crash Course* in December 2019. By then they had both been watching Samuel Leeds' YouTube videos, but Ibby was reluctant to go.

"I said it was in London and we hadn't got the time, but Huslen said, 'No, we're going,'" Ibby remembers.

That determination changed the course of their lives, setting them both on the path to becoming property entrepreneurs. Now the Liverpool-based husband and wife team are making thousands of pounds a month from renting out properties owned by other people.

After joining Samuel Leeds' academy, they also began packaging and selling investment deals, banking more than £10,000 in finder's fees in just a few months. Ironically, at first the couple had doubts about joining up, believing it was too good to be true that money could be made in this way.

Although they had enjoyed the crash course, they decided against signing up for further training at that point.

"We were telling ourselves we hadn't got the money when we did and really wanted it. A poor mentality was still holding us back," admits Ibby.

Huslen was concerned that the creative property investment strategies which they were hearing about sounded unbelievable.

"When Samuel Leeds spoke at the course about selling deals and controlling properties, we were like, really? We kept thinking it was too good to be true."

That scepticism was reinforced by her upbringing.

"I've never had a rich family. I just thought you have to work hard and make money. You can't just make money that easily. If it is you have to pay something back one way, or another."

Despite their reservations, they were both impressed by the crash course and returned twice to absorb the atmosphere.

"We just loved the energy that we got from the events and Samuel," explains Huslen.

After picking up tips from attending the crash courses and studying the videos, Ibby and Huslen managed to secure a lease option. Under this arrangement, they would pay the landlord a fixed monthly fee and then rent out the property as a single let at a higher rate to make a profit. Then, if it worked out, they could exercise their option to buy it down the line. However, they backed out because they were still unsure of their ground.

Around this time, Ibby was working for a sports company and Huslen was looking after their children, aged one and two, and feeling constrained by her circumstances.

"When we planned the kids, I just thought I was going to be a good mum and look after them well. But I struggled and struggled. I just couldn't get out of the house. I was lying in my bed a lot of the time. I went through a really low stage. I was thinking, I'm lucky right to have a kid? It's almost like you shouldn't struggle.

"I tried to do everything by myself and still try to do property on the side. I wasn't getting any help because I just thought it's my responsibility. I have to do this. I know a lot of mums go through this as well."

Her daily routine included cooking, which she felt she could not do, and looking after her children.

"I felt like I was stuck. I was going to go crazy. I couldn't be a stay-at-home mum. I know people love that, but I couldn't."

It was when she became involved in property investing that her mental health improved and she was able to recover her equilibrium.

"One day I thought I'm waiting for Ibby to make money and to become rich and I just said to myself, do you know what, I'm going to be that rich person."

It was that powerful motivation which drove her on to be successful in business after Huslen and her husband also attended a course about unlocking personal potential. Later on, they found a rent-to-rent property to take on, but the months went by, and it failed to perform well.

Eventually, Ibby attended the Property Investors' *Deal Sourcing Mastery* course, while Huslen stayed with their children in a hotel five minutes away from the venue.

"That was a big turning point for me," he says. "The energy was amazing, and I learnt so many new things."

Ibby then decided joining the Property Investors Academy would enable them to progress and give them both the lifestyle they yearned for.

"I had some money in cryptocurrency. I thought even if I do well in that, I'm still going to be working and not having enough time, but if I invest it into skills and trying to give myself more free time I'm going to be in a completely different situation.

"I wanted the potential to grow a lot further. So, for me it was 100 per cent worth it. We'd got the right people around us and nothing was going to stop us now."

Nurtured by the academy coaches, Huslen and Ibby put together a plan of what they wanted to achieve. Their business approach from the outset was based on how they could be of help to someone, whether that was an estate agent or a cleaner.

Ibby says: "We started ringing landlords and saying, 'I see you've got a spare room. I can find a tenant for you. Give me two weeks' rent but I'll find them for you.' And Huslen would go in there to dress the room and market it a lot better and she'd find a tenant."

"That was the point where I realised we could provide value and get paid for it," adds Huslen.

Ibby points out that people presume they know where a bad area is and will not invest in it, but his experience in Liverpool has shown him that it is best to avoid having preconceived ideas.

"I learnt to go on facts rather than assumptions because in some of these areas where we were finding tenants there was actually good demand.

"For HMOs you've got to find out the supply and demand in all of the postcodes of the city to see which areas get tenants really fast and where you can easily fill the rooms."

With their confidence bolstered, one of the landlords Huslen was working with, offered them the chance to manage one of his rental properties. It was a nine-bed, licensed rent-to-HMO in Liverpool which had been not been doing well during the pandemic.

The Rahmans jumped at the chance, even though there were only two tenants when they took control of it from the landlord, who was too busy to run it himself.

Huslen admits they struggled for the first two months to fill the accommodation. So, she dressed up the rooms, bringing in new bedding including 'nice' pillows. Her efforts bore fruit.

"We pay this landlord £1,750 a month and make a profit of £1,000 a month," she says.

In keeping with their stated business aim of adding value, they let the tenant keep the bedding.

Huslen says: "I know some people take it back after the tenants have signed the contract, but we add value to them. We also give them a welcome pack, shampoos, toiletries and fruit – we're healthy landlords."

They advertise their rooms on Airbnb and Facebook, and also hand out promotional leaflets.

"On Airbnb, we'll have a room which we'll list with a minimum stay of 60 days. What usually happens is that we'll get international students or people moving from different countries. For example, we've got one guy from Uzbekistan coming over to Liverpool to work in a hospital," says Ibby.

They charge £350 to £550 a month per room, putting up the rent by a small amount each time a tenant leaves to keep up with price increases. They also ensure they stay proactive with their marketing.

Huslen says: "We contact international people because it's hard for them to come to a new country and settle down. We help with that process, telling them what they need to do for their visa and where they can find cheap taxis."

Ibby defines managing rent-to-serviced accommodation as taking over a whole property and letting it out for short stays. The landlord could run it himself but there are so many advantages of allowing someone else to do that.

"The landlord could be losing money with letting agents, paying them a management and tenant fee every time someone moves out. They also have to do a refurbishment every time someone leaves and there are void periods.

"So, if they get someone in there doing rent-to-rent and taking it all on, it takes off all the hassle and they've got a fixed rent coming in each month. They can walk away from it. We don't have any tenants' rights as well, so it gives him that extra security. They can just kick us out. The accommodation is kept to a much higher standard too."

Ibby and Huslen found their other rent-to-serviced accommodation properties through building a rapport with letting agents. Huslen follows her mentor Samuel's advice closely when assessing the potential profitability of a property.

"Every week whatever he says I just do it because I believe in him 100 per cent."

The pair, who met in a gym eight years ago, back this up with their own methods to visualise whether a deal is a good one or not.

Ibby explains: "We call it the three M's. You need to work out whenever you go through any rent-to-rent deal the maximum amount of capital you want to put down. We don't want to put more than £5,000 into a deal for the furniture, first month's rent, deposit and decoration.

"The next M is the minimum amount of profit you're willing to make. For us it's £500.

"The last one is months. We want to get our money back in under six months. If the deal doesn't stack up straight away – maybe we're not getting back our money until 10 months – then we look at how to reduce our initial capital. Maybe we can get a grace period, or we need to get the furniture on a lease.

"We figure out a strategy to make the property work and then we use that and put it into the offer. It gives you a lot of clarity."

This formula has served them well so far, judging by the average profit for the serviced apartments they control.

Huslen says: "Samuel told us that if you have a 50 per cent occupancy rate – so you have guests only coming in for 15 days – you should still cover your costs. But with our deals we don't just break even at 50 per cent, we make a profit on that."

On one, Ibby adds, the average occupancy rate is 55 per cent and they are making £1,800, while on the other one the profit is £1,200.

It dawned on Huslen just how well they were doing recently. "We were at one of Samuel's events the other day when I received a notification on my phone. It said three nights, £450. Someone had paid already, and I was like, wow I'm just making money while I'm sitting here. The things I wanted are coming true."

Ibby and Huslen have also sourced, negotiated and sold four rent-to-HMO serviced accommodation investment opportunities, as well as selling deals which other people have brought to them.

Huslen is now full-time in property, and Ibby has got support so that he no longer needs to work. He dreams of becoming a trainer himself, while Huslen has formed a help group for mums in property on social media. These days she wakes up excited at what the next day will bring.

"Through property I've met so many amazing people. It's making me money and given me friends. I've got a different lifestyle now. I love working and I want to manage more properties."

Samuel cannot praise the couple enough. He says: "Huslen and Ibby have achieved so much in the last three or four months and they're such an asset to the academy. They give so much. In fact, in their whole business, with their tenants, landlords and agents, they're always thinking of what they can give. They deserve everything they've achieved."

IBBY AND HUSLEN'S TIPS

"When you call a letting agent, don't just ask them straight away if they do rent-to-rent because some of them don't understand it. You need to develop the art of conversation and it will open doors."

"Rent-to-rent isn't passive income. It's only passive for the landlord."

"A lot of people look at deals and say it doesn't work, but we look how to make it work."

Chapter 20 – Doug Juru

Property millionaire with a powerful 'why' joins academy to up his profits

Property Investors' multi-millionaire founder Samuel Leeds has been quoted as saying that he is never going to reach a point where he declares he has achieved enough. He is always pursuing the next property deal and trying to grow his business. His motivation, however, is not the money. It is about being 'the best version of myself.'

At the heart of his mission as a Christian entrepreneur is the overriding desire to leave a legacy which helps his family and the wider community.

This is something Doug Juru can identify with, having become successful in his own right through business and having a strong faith too. Doug set up his first company before Samuel Leeds was even born and amassed a portfolio of around a dozen buy-to-lets, becoming a property millionaire in the process.

His total income from rents amounts to £6,000 a month, making him financially independent. And yet despite this success, he joined the Property Investors Academy to learn how to up his profits.

That might sound odd, but the Zimbabwe-born businessman has a personal reason for wanting to boost his cashflow. With the additional revenue, he plans to return to his homeland to help alleviate poverty.

Doug knows what it is like to be poor himself. When he came to the UK as a young man, he had nothing. He emigrated because at the time his country was ravaged by war and there were no opportunities.

On his arrival, he discovered most people made a living by having a job. Doug is quick to emphasise there is nothing wrong with doing that, but it was not for him.

"I realised the more I became an employee for somebody else all I had was a pay cheque. Sadly, I found I couldn't even last a month with that pay cheque. That was when I decided to go into business."

Starting out in 1984, his first move was to build a nursing home. That was when, Doug says he fell in love with property.

"It went very well because I bought a disused property with no roof, no walls, nothing. Everyone laughed at me. My friends said no, don't do it, but I had found an opportunity. I built it to over £1m worth of property by the time I finished with it."

With the money he made, he began buying properties and rented them out as single lets. One of his first properties was purchased off plan in 2007.

Some 15 years later, Doug, who also runs a network marketing business, happened to be searching YouTube when he saw a video about Evans Willie, who had just won *The Eviction*, Property Investors' annual competition for budding entrepreneurs.

Doug had known Evans for several years and taught him about network marketing. So, when Doug heard that his one-time pupil was practically a millionaire, it made him question his own property strategy. It also inspired Doug to seek out Evans' teacher as he was clearly teaching him well. It was this that led him to Samuel Leeds and his training academy which he joined in January 2022.

When Doug came on to the training programme, he had regrets about not investing more in education over the years.

"That to me was the biggest mistake I ever made, not having enough knowledge. My second one was I didn't really have the focus. My eyes were on other things that I was doing. Because I love personal development, I was focusing more on developing other people not realising I could be developing that as well as the property."

It was quickly brought home to Doug that he had a lot to learn, even though he had been investing in real estate for years. One example of this was when Samuel told his students they should be making a minimum profit of £500 per property. Doug was surprised because his properties were not generating this figure.

He still wishes he had known years ago about the creative strategies available to investors to achieve better returns but refuses to dwell on that.

"I could have done more with what I had but it doesn't matter. I've got to look to the future. I feel I'm just starting out again in property and that's exciting. I want to see how much I can excel because right now I feel nowhere near to my potential."

He adds: "I came from a country in Africa which was very poor. I've never forgotten my roots. For example, people are drinking dirty water which is killing a lot of them and there are other diseases. I think I owe it to my family back home to do what I can here and then to return and help my people."

It is that powerful incentive which keeps him hungry for more success as he looks at how to adapt his portfolio so that the focus is on cashflow as well as capital appreciation.

"My plan for this year is to sit down with my mentors to look at what I've got so we can begin to restructure. There is a lot of potential with the properties I've got but I'm putting the wrong strategies into these properties. Having single lets is OK but it's not where I want to be."

Doug believes it is important to have a reason for wanting to be in property.

"To me it's everything. The energy I get today is more than I've ever had before, especially now I've found an opportunity with the Samuel Leeds organisation. I can see what I could do with more to help other people."

Having an excellent team around him to teach him new skills is crucial. At the academy, he receives a year of coaching, mentoring and support from Samuel Leeds and his team. He also has access to a weekly Mastermind Zoom call when members can share their triumphs and challenges and get instant feedback.

Other benefits include help with preparing a business plan and two days of coaching with Samuel on the best way to achieve personal goals. Doug takes inspiration from his mentor-in-chief.

"I love Samuel's energy and he's always pictured in action. Samuel lights up the room as soon as he walks in because of his energy. I can never have enough of him as a mentor."

Doug also constantly reads up on the subject, enabling him to easily reel off pearls of wisdom from business gurus.

'You can go fast if you run on your own, but you can go further with a team,' is one saying he quotes and: 'TEAM – together everyone achieves more."

In Samuel, he recognises a fellow reader of the same books which enlighten and spur him on.

"He is somebody I admire. He is a very well-read person. It comes out in lectures. I can see the book he's talking about, not by name but by bringing out quotations and information. Leaders are readers. Without that I wouldn't be where I am today."

Doug is keen to push himself as far as he can go in property.

"I have a passion to see how much I can excel at it because by me succeeding I'm going to touch a lot of other people.

"I'm not using all the energy mentally and physically that God has given me to achieve. So, that's why I say I'm just at the beginning."

Doug agrees with Samuel that in the property industry there is the opportunity to 'scale it big' which makes him an enthusiastic student, looking forward to seeing how he can develop his business.

The businessman is learning how to maximise the yield on his portfolio through strategies such as buy, refurbish, refinance and rent which would allow him to pull out money for more investments. Other options open to him include renting out his properties as furnished accommodation for short stays or converting them into HMOs to boost his earnings.

He is also being trained in assessing deals – a vital skill for any property entrepreneur.

"It needs to be a win-win situation for me and the person I'm buying from. It's got to make sense. What value can I get from that deal? Is it good for me? Am I going to get the income I want?"

So far, his property journey has been virtually trouble-free, even though he has many tenants and can therefore expect to have problems from time to time.

"I've always relied on letting agents to manage the tenant side of the business because I didn't have the time or know-how. I'm lucky that I've only had one tenant who's given me any challenges."

Nevertheless, having mental toughness is something he believes is a critical part of being able to succeed in business – that and being 'humble' in looking to others for advice.

"I haven't got to know everything, so bringing in experts has always been my channel of success."

Before becoming a member of the academy Doug spent £6,000 on some online training, but felt it failed to give him the support he needed. That put him off seeking more education for a while until he met Samuel.

From his previous experience, he was sceptical about what he would get out of it but is now convinced of its value.

"As I'm on the training I begin to see success upon success upon success. I'm thinking: 'I'm not better than anybody else but nobody is better than me.'

"One of the coaches has helped me a lot. He said I was looking at too many things. All these strategies were just too many for me. I should find one and focus on that."

Summing up his aim in property, Doug says:

"One thing I'm looking for is to be a person of meaning or significance in life. To have a car, a house and to go on holiday for me is not what it's all about. My mission is to make this world a better place in a small measure than the world I find myself in."

He adds: "I don't look back any more. I've got to look ahead and find a way to get where I want to be."

Samuel has been impressed by the way his student has applied himself. He says: "I can be in a room with 100 people at a free seminar and most of the guys in the room have no properties and are not making any money from property. Doug is there on the front row. He is more motivated than nearly everybody else, even though he's already got a £1m portfolio – in fact much more than that – but he's still hungry. I think that's because he has got a powerful why.

"People think they'll retire when they make £3,000 or £4,000 a month passive income but actually human beings are meant to be continually progressing and growing. If you're not growing, you're dying. Doug is someone who's been in property longer than I have been in this world but even today he has this fire in his belly and is learning and growing. It's really inspiring."

Samuel agrees that having a mentor to guide you is important.

"One of thing things I look for in a mentor is who they have they mentored before and what has the fruit been. Where are the students who have succeeded as a result of that course or that book or that seminar, or teacher? And, of course, I look at how long have they been in the industry. Have they got proof of that? Having a trainer who has energy is important too. You have to go on your intuition as well."

DOUG'S TIPS

"If you're starting out in property, you've got to have a reason for wanting to do it. That's important. Fads don't last two minutes."

"There's a lot of help around. Ask somebody. Once you can find information the road ahead is so plentiful."

"Have a plan of action of where you're going and follow that plan."

"You need a mentor. Look for someone who is walking the walk, like Samuel."

"To find a power team search for people who share the same values as you."

Chapter 21 – Ollie Clarke and Jamie Mcdonald

World class strongman shows his strengths as a deal sourcer in link-up with childhood pal

Childhood friends Ollie Clarke and Jamie Mcdonald were given an in-depth overview of deal sourcing at one of Samuel Leeds' *Discovery Days* which he hosts regularly at his home. Straight away they were hooked by the possibility of making 'big' money fast and enrolled on the academy.

The pair proved to be quick learners. Just a few months after joining up, they were already making around £15,000 a month from selling investment opportunities in the housing market. Since then, Ollie and Jamie have gone from strength to strength as their knowledge has increased. They specialise in packaging and selling buy, refurbish, and refinance deals to wealthy clients and are now looking at taking on their own projects, as well as managing them for others.

It is what they always dreamed of doing when they were boys – being their own bosses and 'earning lots.' Ollie, 21, and Jamie,20, have known each other since the age of five. They attended the same school and as they grew older began looking at ways of making money together.

It was Ollie, a strongman champion, who spotted Samuel Leeds' YouTube channel and started studying his videos. This went on for at least three years as Ollie lapped up the information and urged his friend to watch the videos too.

"Once we left school, Ollie was saying to me all the time we've got to get into property, and he kept showing Samuel to me," recalls Jamie.

Soon they were both hooked on the idea, having convinced themselves this was where their future lay. Again, it was Ollie who found out about the Property Investors Academy and came up with a plan of what they needed to do to achieve their ambition of becoming rich through business.

Fresh out of sixth form, they began saving to pay for the year-long academy programme which gives students the technical and practical skills needed to become successful property entrepreneurs. They worked hard, each holding down more than one job to put by as much cash as they could. Jamie found employment in the trade as a painter and worked in a gym as well, while Ollie, who frequently competes in major strongman contests, was a personal trainer. He also set up an online coaching company which is still operating to supplement his income.

It was an exhausting schedule but their efforts were rewarded. After two years the pals went along to the *Discovery Day*, where they were able to meet their mentor Samuel and pick his brains about everything to do with property investing. Impressed by what they had seen and heard, Ollie and Jamie used their savings to sign up on the day for the advanced training with the Property Investors Academy. After just two months, Jamie gave up his painting job to become a deal sourcer and Ollie is full-time too now.

Jamie says they chose to package and sell property investment deals because it seemed so lucrative.

"There's so much opportunity to make a lot of money and it's fast as well.

There are a lot of strategies in property that are long-term wealth builders, but they take time. Deal selling was the quickest."

Jamie's definition of the strategy is straightforward: "Deal sourcing is finding an investment deal for an investor, packaging it up, getting an offer accepted and passing it on for a fee for ourselves."

The packaging part includes negotiating the price on a property and making sure the figures stack up so that the customer can see what their return on investment is likely to be. Education and mindset are what separate a professional deal sourcer from an amateur in Ollie's opinion.

"Some people just watch a few YouTube videos about property and try to sell deals, but they don't know how to do proper diligence. They don't really know how to sell a deal or the legal side of it," he says.

Assuming they have invested their time and money into becoming properly trained, Jamie's advice to newcomers is to tell everyone about the service they are offering.

"The first step is just telling everyone what you do. People need to know what you're doing to be successful. You can't just try to go undercover. Even if you go and have a haircut, just tell everybody what you do. You don't know who you're going to meet.

"Ollie met someone the other day at Tesco and got chatting to them. Now we're speaking to them properly about it. It's just having that conversation with someone. You don't know what they could bring to you."

This is one of the key messages Samuel preaches to his academy students. Telling the world what they do for a living could give them that all-important lead which turns into a deal. It could connect them to someone who wants to invest their capital or has a property to sell.

On the training Jamie and Ollie were also taught the importance of building a brand to make themselves stand out from the crowd. As a result, they started putting out more content on social media, including documenting their property viewings and deals on sites like TikTok, Instagram and Facebook. They also created their own YouTube channel, called *The Property Guys*, to promote their bespoke deal sourcing service.

"It just came to us on the spot and we both agreed to it," says Jamie.

Publicising themselves on TikTok has already made them money.

Ollie says: "We got a message on TikTok one day. A guy's father had come down ill, so he wanted to sell one of his buy-to-lets. He asked us if we thought we'd be able to sell it. We spoke to some of our investors and managed to sell it in a couple of hours. We charged him £2,000 for that deal. It was off market."

Jamie draws a clear distinction between his role as a 'middle-man' and that of an estate agent.

"A deal sourcer is trying to get the lowest possible price for their investor and the estate agent is trying to get the best possible price for the seller."

If he negotiates £10,000 off the asking price this alone justifies his commission.

Jamie and Ollie's charges vary depending on the size of the deal.

"On average you're looking at one to two per cent of the house price, but it depends on the deal. If you've got a deal that could make £100,000, you might want to charge more."

For a basic deal, they charge a 'finder's fee' of £3,000 to £4,000. This factors in the amount of time spent on the ground researching the market.

The business partners decided early on in their journey that their niche would be to identify houses in need of renovation which could be improved and then refinanced. Ideally, they are looking for properties suitable for conversion into an HMO or serviced accommodation. The investor can then pull out all or most of what they spent on the house by remortgaging it. This gives them cash in their hand to plough into other schemes. At the same time, they benefit from a high level of rent, plus the capital appreciation if it goes up in value again down the line.

"Everyone wants a BRR right now, especially a BRR to HMO or SA. Obviously, it's going to be worth so much more with a commercial valuation," says Jamie.

They target rundown properties which they can obtain below market value and refurbish to make them worth more. Once the work is finished, the property is refinanced with a 75 per cent loan-to-value mortgage based on the new valuation.

"This means you can pull all the money you've put into the project back out. Essentially, you've got the property for free in a roundabout way and then you're just living off the passive income of the rent. That's why people love it."

The last deal they sold was for a three-bedroom terraced house which will be turned into a two-bed flat and a studio apartment and then rented out.

Ollie and Jamie will be supervising the work after speaking to the council to secure grants of £40,000 for the refurbishment.

"The grants are only payable back when you go to sell it, so it was great for our investors. We are also offering project management so that they can be totally hands off," Ollie points out.

As deal sourcers, they package and present an opportunity. It is up to the investor to pay for a survey on a house and find a solicitor to carry out the necessary searches. Even so, Ollie and Jamie will intervene if problems are discovered which suddenly make the property less desirable.

For example, if it was full of damp which had been covered up and was going to cost tens of thousands of pounds to eradicate they would take steps to rectify the situation.

"Our reputation is important, so we would just offer a replacement," explains Ollie. "We'd go out and find a like for like. Things do go wrong sometimes. That's why you have contracts. Everyone's got to be clear from the start what the expectations are.

"It's important as well that you've got the 14-day cooling off period after they've paid you, not to spend that money in case something happens, and you need to give them a refund."

They are registered with the Property Ombudsman and have the required anti-money laundering measures and insurances in place to protect their customers, as well as them.

The two friends posted on social media that they were earning an average of £15,000 a month from deal sourcing. Jamie says they upped that figure to just over £16,000 in January 2022 and now have two bespoke clients in the West Midlands.

"We've been working with them closely to understand their specific needs," adds Ollie. "They want deals up there and we'll be looking for properties for them. Every day we'll be in and out of agents and ringing agents.

"It's a fun life, different than from a normal office, nine-to-five job."

Jamie and Ollie are based in Essex/Hertfordshire and have had a few deals there but compared to other regions it is not as good for property and return on investment, they say. So, they have been going further afield, not just to the West Midlands but across the border to Wales as well.

Manchester, Liverpool, Newcastle and Durham are also rich hunting grounds. Competition in the market is stiff due to the dearth of houses being put up for sale. For that reason, they make an offer on the same day they view a property, if they are interested in it.

They have also established relationships with estate agents so that they are offered properties before they are advertised on sites like Rightmove.

When not on the road, they work from 8am to 5pm in a room converted into a large office in Ollie's house.

Ollie, who won the title of Under 23 UK Strongest Man in 2020, says that their aim is to be financially free so they can do whatever they want and control their earnings.

"I was earning £4,000 to £5,000 a month but it was constant working. I want the money from property to be able to push my strongman sport as far as I can."

Jamie was making £3,000 to £3,500 a month but had to work seven days a week to earn that. He is also driven by the desire to 'be the best' and to follow a different route to the usual one of going to university and getting a job. He has another motivation.

For two years he has been growing his hair so that he can shave it off for the charity CALM – the Campaign Against Living Miserably - which is seeking to bring down the high level of suicides in the UK, particularly among men.

"Men's mental health is a big issue today. It's something a lot of people go through, and they don't speak about it. I've gone through it myself. It's harder for men to speak about it. That's why we need to bring more awareness to the problem.

"Property has certainly affected our lives positively. There's always a reason to wake up now. There's always something going on with us, a goal in mind."

Samuel believes they are capable of going even further in property. He says: "Ollie and Jamie have taken the business seriously by joining the Property

Investors Academy. They're on all the training programmes, the mentoring calls, sessions and the Mastermind groups. It's also good for networking.

"Now they're earning far more than what they used to and doing what they love with opportunities to scale up and invest in projects. They're working smart, making crazy money, but even so they don't have to put their profits into their own deals. They can joint venture."

OLLIE AND JAMIE'S TIPS

"Jamie: If you're starting out as a property investor, get yourself out there. Take advantage of social media. It's such a big part of today's society. It's hard to keep up but you need to do it."

"Ollie: "Get the knowledge and once you've mastered everything just go out and do it."

*At the time of publication Ollie is dedicated all his time to his biggest ambition – becoming the ultimate strongman champion. He says he would have been unable to focus purely on training in this 'make or break' year had it not been for the success he gained in his property venture.

Chapter 22 – Mark and Martin Pow

Brothers make £109,000 in one deal alone after training with Samuel Leeds

It took Mark and Martin Pow 12 years to build up their HMO portfolio and just 12 months to pull off a string of development deals, including one earning them more than £100,000 annually.

They credit Samuel Leeds with helping them to speed up their progression and increase their profits. Even though the brothers were already property millionaires, they invested £10,000 in training with Samuel and his coaches to learn new ways of making money from real estate.

Since then, Martin and Mark have gone into overdrive to expand their business using creative strategies, as well as other people's funds in some cases. One of their biggest triumphs was securing a lease option agreement on a hotel which they converted into serviced accommodation. In 2021/22, that one deal alone made them £109,000 and they expect a similar income from it moving forward.

The entrepreneurs are also about to embark on a joint venture project with a projected seven-figure pay-off and have other developments on the go which they hope will cement their success.

It was during lockdown that Mark and Martin began watching Samuel's YouTube videos and realised there were other strategies they could be using to boost their revenue. Soon afterwards they signed up for the Property Investors' *Development Mastermind* course.

As a result, they have been 'absolutely smashing it,' as Mark describes it, because it taught them that they could draw on other people's assets and resources to grow their portfolio. Until the pair came on the course, they had always used their own cash to invest in property. That was how they became financially independent, buying and doing up houses which they then rented out as HMOs.

Each one was refinanced after being renovated, giving them capital to reinvest in the next property.

Mark says joining forces with his younger brother worked well.

"We did all the work ourselves and then slowly we've been getting bigger and bigger HMOs as we've gone on."

They had a head start in the business. Martin is a carpenter by trade, while Mark also had transferable skills after previously working in car sales. With just two of them involved, however, it was a slow process completing each project. They were limited too by how much money they had at their disposal which was why it took so long to acquire their six HMOs.

Five of their properties are in Newton Abbot in Devon where they grew up. They also have a house share in Torquay which is where they clinched their 'big money' hotel deal.

Mark and Martin planned initially to buy it as a commercial building, but then it was down valued. Rather than just walking away, the brothers sought alternative ways of purchasing the hotel, using the knowledge they had gained from their training.

"That's when we thought what's the solution for this? Let's go down the route of a PLO (Purchase Lease Option)," explains Mark.

The owner had been struggling to sell the hotel, recalls Martin, and they were eager to get their hands on it because they knew they could make 'good money' out of it. The arrangement, therefore, worked well for both parties.

Martin and Mark became aware of the lease option strategy through studying Samuel's free YouTube content and reading books on the subject.

Defining the method, Mark says: "A lease option is where you control a building normally with a very small deposit, hopefully £1. You then control that building for x amount of time, generally for approximately five years, sometimes longer, sometimes shorter, with the option but not the obligation to purchase it at the end of the agreement."

Having sealed the PLO agreement, Mark and Martin wanted to turn the hotel into an HMO because it had 13 bedrooms, all with en suites, but could not obtain planning permission. So instead they decided to offer it as serviced accommodation.

"In the end it was a blessing in disguise. We're making more money out of it now than we would have done if it was an HMO," says Martin.

They rent out the rooms through Airbnb or booking.com on a day-by-day basis which has helped drive up their takings.

"It's generating a profit of just over £9,000 a month at the moment," Mark says.

Martin adds: "It was a good feeling, after all that hard work, seeing the first few bookings coming in and they then just literally kept coming."

Whilst many people would be tempted to retire on their income from just that one property transaction, the brothers have no intention of winding down just yet. In fact, there is no limit to their ambitions to climb even further up the property ladder.

"We're quite driven people. We haven't really got an end goal," Martin admits.

Mark and Martin's furnished accommodation in Torquay is not only giving them an excellent rental yield, it will also release investment funding.

"We'll get a commercial mortgage on the property, pull all the money out that we invested, plus probably another £100,000 to £110,000," Mark points out.

Soon after completing the work on that scheme, they had an offer accepted on a three-bed semi-detached house. Despite competition for houses, they managed to negotiate the price down from £250,000 to £215,000.

Martin believes the fact it was divided into three flats meant a lot of people overlooked it, giving them the opportunity to submit a 'cheeky offer.'

Their plan is to spend £30,000 on refurbishing the property, including changing the kitchen and bathroom to improve the look of it. Once the work is finished, they expect the end valuation to be around £350,000. After refinancing the mortgage to the new value of the house, this will enable them to pull out just over £100,000 and take rents from the three flats.

In addition to that, they have secured a Grade II listed building which they plan to revamp by creating nine flats in the space, subject to planning consent. They are also hoping to get the go ahead on another Purchase Lease Option to turn a commercial building into a six-bed HMO.

"It's a bit smaller than we generally want but we're just waiting for them to come back and say yay. By the sound of things everything's a goer," says

Mark.

Going forward, their efforts will be concentrated on land development and commercial to residential conversions. They see this as their natural progression as they scale up and go 'bigger and bigger.'

Their seven-figure scheme is one example of this. They were approached to take it on after Mark gave some advice to a friend who was considering purchasing a hotel in Torquay.

"I wasn't trying to jump on the deal. I was just helping him out. It didn't go through for him sadly. That was about six months ago. Then earlier this month he contacted me and said: 'I've got this. Do you want to jump on and help us out?' It's a joint venture."

Their last two projects have been joint venture deals. Mark says they will only take 50 per cent of the profit but that is 'better than zero.'

Martin adds: "The plan is to develop and sell on, take out the profit and then hopefully get a few more projects. We've got two on the go now."

So far very few of their deals have come about through them actively calling agents. Instead, they have relied on Rightmove and word of mouth to find their properties. They acknowledge this needs to change.

Mark says: "We've only just started branding ourselves. We've been very quiet about what we do and have done. There are quite a few friends who don't actually know we're in property at all. We're going to have to start doing that [publicising themselves].

"The thing that's been holding us back is that we've only used our own cash to build our property business. The whole idea now is to build with joint venture people so we can scale our business and make both us and our partners a ton of money."

Their goal for the coming year is to get 10 development deals with JV partners. The brothers are keen to locate land they can build houses on.

They have already been tramping through fields looking at potential sites and will also be ringing estate agents to help them identify plots before they come on the market.

Martin says his training with Property Investors has shown him how to recognise a bad deal and avoid wasting time on researching a development possibility which is likely to be refused at the planning stage – because there is no access, for example, or there are protected trees on the land.

He has also benefited from the way Samuel and his team teach their students, giving them practical exercises as well as the theory.

"I find it very motivating. We've done training before. In a classroom environment I just struggle and switch off. I'm not very good in that situation but with Samuel's training I felt I was in the room all the time. It was so easy to soak up the information.

"It's also been good to be around the same people as yourself. You keep in contact with them and then you're doing deals and they are. It's just nice to see what's going on around us as well."

Mark agrees: "It is the whole ethos of everybody, the training, the other students on the course. It brings everybody up. It really motivates you.

"I wish I'd known what I do now ten years ago."

He feels they have had excellent value for their money.

"It might seem a lot spending £10,000 on the *Development Mastermind* course but then if you do one deal and make £100,000 that's 10 per cent of your first deal and you can do lots of deals. It's nothing."

They can also call Samuel and his trainers for advice and bounce ideas off them.

Martin and Mark originally went into property to make money but now having time with their families is the priority.

"When we started no one ever thought Covid would exist and then as time has gone on our plan has changed," says Mark. "We've both got young children. We now value time over money a lot more, to be able to spend time with the kids and family just enjoying life. Part of that is not having to worry about money."

Samuel says: "What Martin and Mark's experience shows is that if you invest into a deal, you've got to wait for that deal to be finished. It could be as long as three years before you can pull your money out which means you're only working on one deal at a time.

"Whereas if you're using other people's money you can do five to 15 deals all in one go and ultimately make a lot more money, as well as help other people do the same thing. I'm really pleased with what Mark and Martin have achieved and honoured to have played a part in their journey. What they've done in a year is more than most people would do in a lifetime. Their portfolio is now worth millions which is incredible."

MARK AND MARTIN'S TIPS

"Connect with people. We've found the bigger we get the less it is about the property and it's more about the network around you. We're now heavily focusing on JV's so that we can build our property portfolio. We've also got a good power team."

"It's best to start small and work your way up. We've done that and got a nice cashflow coming in. It gives you that security so that when you want to jump on to the bigger stuff you can."

"Do the training and take action. As Samuel says, you're either going to pay for your education or your mistakes."

"In property you find there are roadblocks and different routes to get to the end destination. You need to know all the avenues you can take so that if something doesn't work you can find alternative solutions. You might even be able to make a better profit."

Chapter 23 – Ondrej Liska and Vincent Hovorka

Brothers-in-law are now serving hungry investors instead of café customers

Brothers-in-law Vincent Hovorka and Ondrej Liska had virtually no money when they decided to go into property. So, they harnessed other people's funds and assets to gain a foothold in the industry, using strategies taught to them by Property Investors' coaches.

These days Vincent and Ondrej are enjoying the fruits of their labours after establishing a bulging portfolio of rental properties. In total they control seven rent-to-rent serviced accommodation units, plus two single lets and have also completed a buy, refurbish, refinance project. Topped up with selling property deals, their average income amounts to a healthy £6,000 a month.

The pair even took out loans to pay for their training. Originally from the Czech Republic and now living in Scotland, Vincent and Ondrej opted to become property entrepreneurs because they were dissatisfied with their lives.

Vincent owned a street food business and café. But despite having a passion for cooking, he felt it was not leading him anywhere. He was working long hours as a chef alongside Ondrej, leaving him with hardly any time to be with his family.

After his two children came along, Vincent realised he needed to change his lifestyle.

"I wanted more freedom. I was spending more time in the business than with them. So, I had to decide to change my life," he explains.

Ondrej was so fed up with what he was doing he ran away to Iceland, staying there for several months. On his return Vincent invited him to come along with him to a three-day Property Investors course in Glasgow.

At that time, Vincent had 'zero minus,' to invest as he puts it, having sunk all his resources into his businesses, and still having to repay loans. With savings of £600, Ondrej was not much better off. Even so, after attending the course they were determined to 'jump into it straight away.'

Their first move was to purchase a property at auction. Not having the time to go to the sale themselves, they submitted a maximum proxy bid of £22,000.

Ondrej laughs when he describes how they discovered their bid had been accepted. "We were driving to the café in the morning when I saw I had a missed call. It was from the auctioneers saying we had won the auction. We were like, oh, OK!"

Ondrej and Vincent now had 28 days to produce the money to complete the acquisition but were faced with first having to find the deposit of £8,000. Someone quickly lent them the cash, but they still had to pay the balance or lose the property.

"It was a stressful month," recalls Vincent. "We were going for meetings with friends and different people, asking for money to invest in the deal.

No one believed us because we were chefs. They said to us, 'What are you going to do with the property?' We said, 'We don't know but we need to do it.' We were pushing so hard. We had to make it work because we'd already borrowed the £8,000."

Finally, they managed to raise the finance and increased the value of the property by refurbishing it.

"It cost £43,000 and the end value was £100,000. So, we were able to pull our money out," Ondrej explains.

It took a year and a half to finish the project after they experienced struggles with builders, but it taught them some key lessons about the process and potential snags. It also proved to be an excellent investment.

Vincent and Ondrej not only managed to effectively obtain a free house by refinancing the mortgage to the new value they also rent it out which gives them a passive income.

"We're getting a rent of £750 a month. The profit on that is £430," says Vincent.

At his *Property Millionaire Intensive* course Samuel Leeds advised the business partners to focus on strategies which would give them 'quick cash,' such as rent-to-rent serviced accommodation and deal selling. So, the entrepreneurs signed up for one of Samuel's *Discovery Days* and followed that up with some more training on lease option agreements.

They then secured two lease options in a month in England.

Ondrej says: "We used the letters Samuel suggested and got a deal in Bradford from it. It worked well. We approached the landlords and got a deal out of it and then a second one."

Vincent's explanation of how the strategy works is straightforward.

"You buy the house now, but you pay for it later. You agree on a price and that's what you can buy it for in a few years' time. The only people you need to pay are the solicitors to draw up the contract.

"We managed to get one of them for seven years and the other one for 10 years. It gives us a lot of time to save for the deposit and buy it, which is good, but we also have an agreement that we can purchase it at any time during the period. So, if the prices go up, we can just buy it tomorrow."

"It's only an option to buy. We don't have to buy it, but if the owner wants to sell, they have to sell it to you," Ondrej interjects.

They travelled over the border to find a lease option agreement because in Scotland they would be obliged to buy the property.

Vincent says the landlord was happy with their proposal because the two properties had been in negative equity.

"Both are single lets. One of them is a joint venture. We are always using other people's money because we don't have any," he says smiling.

One of their lease options brings in £120 a month and the other £230 per month. They are also benefiting from the capital appreciation, having made no investment, other than giving up their time.

In January 2021, the duo started trying to sell property deals to investors to make more 'fast pounds' but without any training they sold none.

Vincent says: "We thought maybe our investor list of 60 people was not enough. We also thought it wasn't working in the locations we were looking at. So, we didn't give up, but we postponed it."

Instead, Vincent and Ondrej concentrated on finding a rent-to-rent arrangement. After watching Samuel Leeds' YouTube videos about the creative strategy, they hit the road to view properties.

With no face-to-face training, however, they floundered until eventually they got their first 'yes' on their first rent-to-rent deal in Durham – after 26 viewings and a similar number of rejections.

As this was something new to them and they would be using money from an investor, they wanted to make sure it would be profitable. So, they enrolled on Property investors' *Never Use Your Money Again* and *Buy, Refurbish, Refinance* courses.

At the training, Samuel asked his students how many rent-to-rents they would need to be financially independent.

"In my head I said I don't need that many. I wrote down my goals and said I wanted to do six in the next three months. We managed to get six in four months," Vincent remembers.

Ondrej and Vincent sold three of the rent-to-rent deals to investors and are managing the properties for them.

Vincent says they are earning an average of around £400 per property each month. "Of course, some of them are joint ventures again because we're not using any of our own money. So, we are sharing the profits.

"From the single lets we are getting £1,000 a month, and £3,000 per month from the rent-to-rents. We started deal sourcing in June 2021 again. We sell one deal a month for around £2,000. It's about £6,000 on average at the moment [in total]."

The two of them have spent thousands of pounds on training, all of which has been funded by investors.

Vincent was attending one Property Investors course when he messaged two people asking them to lend him money for more training.

'I texted one of them, saying can you lend me £1,000? They replied: 'For what?' 'I said, training course. Investing in myself.' Another person the same. I got £2,000 and bought the course."

A waitress friend agreed to help Ondrej. Even with friends, they draw up a contract, he says, because 'everyone wants to have security.'

Vincent agrees: "We have a simple, two-page loan agreement. [It states] how much they're giving us, for how long, and what the rate is. Then it's signed and dated."

Depending on the type of venture they are involved in, they will usually borrow money for a minimum of a year on a monthly interest rate of one per cent.

Vincent emphasises that this is not risky if they know how much profit they are going to be making after doing their research.

"If the rent-to-SA is going to be making £500 a month and someone lends us £5,000 for the deal, for example, we would give them interest of £50 from that. You can put money on the side to pay them for the year. After that you are just profiting without putting any money of your own in."

Ondrej adds: "They may have savings which are not doing anything for them. So, if you offer them some interest on their money, they're happy to lend it to you. If they have some questions, you can always show them the project they're going to invest in. If it makes sense to them, they're happy to go ahead.

"It takes time to build relationships and get people to believe in you and put money into a deal. They need to know and trust you, so obviously that doesn't happen overnight. Having said that I've networked with people through social media. Some I've never met in person but because we've been in touch for several months, they know what sort of person I am."

Initially they simply asked their family and friends for money, but now their approach is more sophisticated. They follow a script, and they know how to 'ask more professionally,' says Vincent.

"You ask them for help to check the project you have and if they know someone who would be willing to invest in it. They're then like, why doesn't he ask me? He doesn't know he is the person we are asking for money.

"The next time I ask them the same. I say, 'I know you're already investing £4,000 in this deal but do you know anyone who would have £3,000 for this deal?' They say, 'I have another £3,000.' Sometimes it is the people we don't think have the money who lend it to us."

Both men are much more satisfied with their lives now that they are full-time property entrepreneurs.

Ondrej says: "We are progressing, and we still want to grow. I feel more fulfilled than before. I'm not depending on someone's pay cheque."

Vincent also feels more fulfilled than when he was running his café.

"I'm doing what I want to do, going to viewings and being around like-minded people if I go networking or do training with Property Investors. I like being in the community. It's a very powerful network. I met joint venture partners on the *Never Use Your Own Money Again* and *BRR* courses. They're still sending me messages now wanting to do joint ventures."

Samuel is full of praise for his students: "Some people might think it sounds too good to be true to be able to build a portfolio with no money but Vincent and Ondrej have proved you can do just that. They started out with nothing and have accumulated all these properties by using other people's money. They've only been doing this for about 18 months which isn't that long. Now they're in a good financial position.

"Ondrej and Vincent made a bold move at the beginning of their property journey by bidding on an auction property without any money. I wouldn't recommend that as it is risky, but they pulled it off and have done remarkably well since."

*Vincent and Ondrej now manage 33 serviced accommodation apartments through their company, Where to Stay Apartments Ltd. They are also sourcing one deal a month on average.

VINCENT AND ONDREJ'S TIPS

"Ondrej: Invest in yourself."

"You have to have goals and push them and also surround yourself with people who have either done it or at least they can show you how to do it."

"Vincent: Don't be afraid to take action, massive action right now."

"The most important thing to do is to build credibility when you're starting out in property. Go networking and advertise your services on social media."

Chapter 24 – Ben Jones

Rubgy fan's decision to swap cup final for the crash course pays off in style

Students of Samuel Leeds are used to hearing him come out with catch phrases as he stands before them sharing his knowledge and expertise. They are designed to motivate them as they take their first steps in property and to encourage them to analyse their approach to life. One of his favourite comments is: 'You can either find excuses or get rich.'

Rugby fan Ben Jones had the perfect get-out for not attending the second day of a *Property Investors Crash Course*. England were taking on giants of the game South Africa in the 2019 world cup final. It was a momentous occasion which might not come round again. He wanted nothing more than to switch on his TV and watch the drama unfold in what promised to be a thrilling contest. But then Samuel reminded his audience of the importance of commitment. So, Ben chose to 'get rich' instead by coming to the crash course.

As it turned out, it was the right decision. England lost the game anyway, but more significantly Ben joined the Property Investors Academy at the event. Two years later he is about to wrap up his eighth buy, refurbish, refinance project in Liverpool. Once it is completed the rents from the properties will bring in around £110,000 a year.

It is an impressive achievement, made more remarkable by the fact that Ben managed to build up the £1.3m portfolio with a friend while holding down a full-time job.

His story of how he got into property investing is one shared by many people who have emerged from the academy to become successful entrepreneurs. His job was no longer fulfilling his needs and so he went in search of something that could give him financial freedom.

For more than a decade Ben depended on his salary from working as an engineer in a contracting business. Then in 2016, a slump in the market led to him being out of work for six months, and again for the same period in 2019.

It was at that point that Ben recognised he had been over reliant on his job and took action to address the problem. He read a book about building wealth through investing in assets, such as real estate, and then searched for a course to give him some ideas.

After googling 'property course London', the name of Samuel Leeds appeared at the top of the search results, along with details of his free crash course.

Ben immediately booked himself on the first event available, not realising it overlapped with the rugby world cup final being held that November.

"I'm a big rugby fan. I didn't know England would be in the final but as it turned out they were. The course was on a Friday and Saturday. Samuel let everyone know that to get anywhere you've got to be committed. I really wanted to watch the game, but I cancelled my plans and came to the course on the second day," Ben remembers.

He was impressed by what he saw: "The crash course was at Earl's Court, with about 1,000 people there. I thought it was powerful that Samuel was able to attract that size of audience and felt there was a lot of value in it. I liked what I heard and that's why I signed up to the academy that weekend. It gave me a great foundation."

By now he was working again and could afford the training with Property Investors. He also viewed it as an opportunity to meet new people and pick up ideas from their deals.

"It's given me a great network and I've also completed the property development course. I've really enjoyed it."

Ben learnt about the strategies available to property entrepreneurs to make money in the housing market. Afterwards he began looking for a patch where he could put his knowledge into practice.

Properties in Southwest London, where he lives, were too expensive, so he headed north to Liverpool where he knew the return on investment was much better.

"One of the houses in our portfolio is worth £90,000. It makes £600 a month in rent. If you times those numbers by ten, there are lots of houses near me for £900,000 but you'd never get £6,000 in rent," says Ben.

Liverpool attracted him because he felt the city had 'something about it.' There were universities and football teams and a lot of developments springing up. All these factors made it an excellent hunting ground for investors like himself.

On one of Samuel's *Discovery Days* at his house he suggested Ben should recycle his money rather than spend £100,000 on two buy-to-lets which would give him a minimal profit. So, Ben began knocking on agents' doors with his business partner to try to clinch a buy, refurbish, refinance deal.

If he could find a run-down house and buy it at a discounted price, he could renovate it and push up its worth. Then the property could be remortgaged to its new value which would give him money to invest in another deal.

It was then that they got lucky. By chance they came across an agent who was helping a client to acquire a portfolio of 50 properties. They were in the hands of a receiver and the buyer wanted to sell some of them to release funds for refurbishing the remaining stock.

"They were really dilapidated. She needed a quick sale as I think she'd bought the whole portfolio using some sort of finance. So, it was quite expensive to her. She was really motivated to sell, and we were motivated to buy. We were in the right place at the right time," Ben explains.

Initially, Ben and his business partner Mike combined their savings to purchase three of the properties for just under £40,000 each to avoid paying stamp duty. The asking price was £40,000 but Ben negotiated the figure down to £39,950. Just by knocking off £50 they saved themselves £3,600.

The cost of refurbishing each one came to around £30,000. Once the work was finished the end valuations came in at £85,000, £90,000 and £92,000. After all the fees were paid, it meant they could pull out 95 per cent of what they had invested. They then repeated the process until they had bought eight properties.

"The eighth one isn't tenanted yet as the refurb is still ongoing. Once that is complete the gross rent annually will be about £110,000. The profit is roughly 50 per cent," says Ben.

One of the biggest challenges for Ben and Mike was 'pulling the trigger' when it came to purchasing the three properties. They wanted to achieve an end valuation of £90,000 but other comparable houses in the area were selling for less.

Doubts set in and they were concerned their margins might be too low. However, they pressed ahead. As the seller wanted to move quickly, they also had to act fast.

"That was one of the biggest things – learning to move quickly and make decisions. You've got to be decisive otherwise you're going to miss the opportunity," says Ben.

He adds: "The builder's quote came in pretty much on the money. There were a couple of little variations but nothing major. He started when he said he was going to start and finished when he said he would. It was ideal."

The sale went through in September 2020 and three months later two of the three properties were tenanted.

As they had owned them for less than six months, there were only a few lenders they could apply to for a mortgage. When the valuations came in, they were told each property was worth what they had paid for it, plus the cost of the refurbishment which came to £70,000.

Disappointed with this estimate, Ben called his mentor Samuel for advice. "I thought this can't be right, but Samuel said my expectations were too high, not on the value but on the timescale."

So, they decided to bide their time, having already bought their fourth property.

"We had the money to do the fourth one. We weren't overly concerned in the sense we were still progressing. So, we just thought we'd wait until we'd owned them for six months."

Their patience was rewarded when another lender gave them a valuation of £90,000.

Ben recognises that whilst he is accumulating wealth through forcing up the equity in a property, the cashflow could be improved.

"Take one of those £90,000 properties. We're probably making £250 to £300 a month. It feels like a lot of time and effort for £300 a month. But it's nice that it's sat there. It should be £300 a month forever.

"You need to do a mix of things. We're focused on BRRs now but maybe we need to think of some other strategies, like Samuel says."

Most of their annual rent roll of £110,000 will come from their HMOs but they started out with some single lets.

"If you do your first one as a BRR HMO, you're going to be limited to a certain number of lenders who do that. We wanted to make sure we had a couple of single lets first. It makes your life easier for the HMOs because you'll open up a wider group of lenders. Also, BRRs tend to be more efficient if they're a single let because there's less to be done to them.

"We've got a four-bed HMO we've refurbed. The amount of money it takes to convert that is quite high relatively. We spent £30,000 refurbing a two up two down. It can cost double that for an HMO because you've got to fit things like fire doors, smoke alarms and en suites.

"You could spend £60,000 to £70,000 converting not exactly the same house but not too far off and then you won't pull all your money out."

On the other hand, the HMOs generate more rent. It's 'swings and roundabouts,' Ben concedes.

"One of the properties we bought was an operating HMO. There is the potential to do it up and probably increase the rent."

When Ben and his partner were buying their houses in 2020, estate agents were warning that the Liverpool property market was about to crash. Their nerves kicked in. However, they were reassured by Samuel's prediction that prices would rise which proved to be the case.

Ben also believed the problems caused by the coronavirus pandemic would be short-lived and there would be a solution.

"When we spoke to agents there was still quite high demand for rentals.

We were targeting families for our single lets, rather than students who'd gone home because of Covid, causing landlords to have voids. So, it didn't feel like it applied to us."

Ben rejected other strategies like rent-to-rent and deal sourcing which generate 'a fast pound,' because he thought he would just be creating another job for himself. Now, with the benefit of experience, deal sourcing may be an option in future.

"We want to think about getting into deal sourcing because you're assessing deals anyway. A deal might not necessarily be appropriate for you, but it could well be appropriate for somebody else. But saying I'm going to quit my job and make that my job, we're not ready for that yet."

They also have another property deal on the cards in London.

"It has got a lot of potential to flip. It's a loft conversion and an extension. It is similar to some of the stuff we've done in Liverpool but it's on a bigger scale. It feels like a natural progression. The work isn't that much different but because of the location it makes it much more lucrative."

His wife helps him pursue his property business alongside his work. They have just had a baby, and she also looks after their other children.

"She's helping me not have to put in time with the kids so I can do this. Obviously, it's for us at the end of the day. Having a partner helps as well. If I go on holiday, Mike looks after things and vice versa."

Samuel is full of praise for his student: "Ben has shown incredible commitment over the past two years. I remember saying there's nothing wrong with watching rugby, but you've got to be rooting for yourself to win. There's never a perfect time to start in property. As I often say, you can either find excuses or get rich. Ben is now a property millionaire. So he made a good decision to complete the crash course."

BEN'S TIPS

"When you're approaching an agent about a BRR deal, just be yourself and have a chat. We call beforehand to make sure there is somebody available to talk to us."

"We've found independent agents are more willing to think out of the box than the High Street ones."

"I've learnt you have to put the hours in as sometimes things can take a little time in property."

Chapter 25 – Destiny Smith-Brown and Jake Carswell

Childhood sweethearts aged just 21 tie up lucrative holiday property business in Bournemouth

Destiny Smith-Brown and Jake Carswell may only be 21 but they are already experienced property entrepreneurs. The childhood sweethearts went into business together in 2019 and now control six rent-to-serviced accommodation units.

The couple clinched their first deal when they were just 18 after attending the *Property Investors Crash Course.* They rang lots of landlords asking if they could rent out their properties until one offered them an apartment a stone's throw from Bournemouth Pier and the beach.

That one flat alone makes them a profit of around £2,000 a month, with their total income from their portfolio projected to increase fivefold during the summer tourist season.

It was Destiny who got them into property investing at the age of 17. She came across Samuel Leeds' YouTube channel while working as an apprentice in an estate agency. Seeing that the Property Investors founder was holding one of his free crash courses in London, she 'dragged' her boyfriend Jake along for moral support.

That was when the pair first heard about the rent-to-SA strategy. The teenagers discovered they could make money by renting out other people's investment homes to holidaymakers. All they had to do was pay the owners a guaranteed monthly rent and look after their properties. Then, they would charge guests a higher rate to stay there and pocket the difference.

As a business model, it made a lot of sense to them as they live in the seaside resort of Bournemouth, which attracts millions of visitors every year.

As Destiny puts it: "A holiday is essential, isn't it?"

With a captive market beckoning, Jake and Destiny decided to put their savings of about £1,000 each into identifying somewhere they could rent out as holiday lets. Their youth and lack of experience weighed against them.

"Landlords didn't take us seriously at all," explains Destiny. "We were basically saying, 'Oh hi. We're 17. Can we rent your property and rent it out please? They would ask what our credentials were, and we had none."

Jake agrees. "When landlords look at you and you're 17, it's like, no chance."

Despite receiving about ten rejections, they persevered. "Samuel told us we were going to be told no a lot, so we thought, right we'll keep going," says Destiny. "Then we finally had a really chilled landlord who said yes, take it for three years. We've still got that one now."

"It's in a perfect location. It's literally a minute's walk from Bournemouth Pier round the corner from nightclubs," Jake adds.

They found the luxury, one-bedroom apartment in a new block of flats on Rightmove and agreed a rent of £750 a month with the agent who took references from their employers. At that point Jake was working for a sports retailer and Destiny was still serving her apprenticeship.

Having used their wages to prove that they could afford the rent, they then obtained the landlord's permission to rent out the flat per night as furnished accommodation for short stays.

"At lunchtimes we were meeting and going to clean the property. We were saying to each other, let's make as much money as possible," recalls Destiny.

Destiny and Jake employ cleaners nowadays, and the rent has gone up to £775 per month, but their margins are still high.

"We make about £2,000 a month profit off that property. It's our best performing one even now. That's after all bills as well," adds Destiny.

Within two years of establishing their enterprise, the partners had two rental units under their control. They also managed to secure a two-bedroom cabin with its own garden and an antique wood burner in the heart of the New Forest. Then at the start of 2022 they took on another four rent-to-rents – including one with the use of an outdoor swimming pool.

During lockdown Destiny was put on furlough for eight months which freed her up to try to expand their operation. After achieveing that aim, she became a full-time property entrepreneur in August 2021. Jake joined her a few months later.

Their holiday lets are in Dorset and Hampshire. As well as the one-bedroom flat and the cabin, they have three studio flats in Bournemouth, one of which sleeps four people, and a two-bedroom apartment with en suite facilities, a large balcony and gated parking a few miles away from Poole Quay.

Their management service includes the initial set-up of the property, advertising it on booking platforms and social media, dealing with enquiries, providing cleaning, as well as welcome packs for their customers.

They concede that they got lucky with their first rent-to-rent but feel they know their trade 'inside out' now.

Destiny's parents are both entrepreneurs. This inspired her to travel all the way to the capital for the *Property investors Crash Course.*

"They've got businesses and I've always thought I'm not working for someone else," she explains.

Jake decided to keep his girlfriend company in the knowledge that it was a free event and he had nothing to lose. That was also their attitude when they went into business.

"I feel, at 17 it was the best time because you don't have a house to lose. You're still living at home. You can put everything you've got into it, starting with £1,000, and you can just make that back," Destiny says.

Their partnership has worked well. "We thought we'd be fighting like cats and dogs but actually we're not," she adds.

Recently, they began working with a landlord/developer who owns multiple properties and has told them they can have as many of his units as they want. In time they intend to take him up on his offer.

Destiny messaged Samuel Leeds on Instagram to thank him for his help after the deal was agreed on the four properties which they took on in 2022 and they had paid the first month's rent.

"I thought I'm going to message Samuel because I didn't even know what the structure of this business was until we went to the crash course. It is all down to Samuel."

Jake says the most challenging part of their journey so far has been having to depend solely on the business for an income after they left their jobs.

"Then with four more properties you're having to put rent and a deposit down. We were pretty much doing it by the skin of our teeth."

Jake and Destiny accept they have no choice other than to 'make it work.' It will be several months before it is clear how much they are making from their latest properties, but already they are anticipating excellent returns.

"From the entire portfolio we expect to make around £10,000 a month. In the summer it will be more because we up our prices. It will be about £10,000 to £12,000 in July I believe. August will probably be about the same," predicts Jake.

During the quieter months the forecast is about £7,000 a month.

Being in property has given them so much more freedom, Destiny believes, although Jake makes the point that they never get a day off as they are 'messaging guests 24/7.'

Destiny acknowledges it is a full-time job but says that when they get a few more rent-to-rents under their belt they will look at hiring someone to help them. The couple, who met at school when they were 16, are also considering signing up for advanced training with Property Investors to learn about other strategies, such as deal sourcing and the buy, refurbish, refinance srategy.

Whilst Destiny comes from a business background, she stresses that neither her parents nor Jake's have contributed financially to their success.

"We haven't had a penny. It's all been our own money that started it. My parents are quite big on if you really need us then we're here, but you need to make your own money."

Jake agrees: "My parents have always been supportive, but I haven't seen one penny. I don't want to. I want to make it myself."

When they made the jump into property, he admits family and friends did not really understand what they were doing.

"Because a lot of them are nine to five that's all they live for. They just look for the pay cheque at the end of the month. There's nothing wrong with that but we like to work for ourselves. We like to get our own money."

Destiny is also convinced that what she is doing is right for them, in spite of what some friends occasionally say.

"When we're up at three in the morning dealing with guests who maybe aren't happy with something they're a bit like ,is it worth it? Is it worth that £100 a night? I reply, 'Yes, it is in the long run.'

"Also, I think with SA what's good is that if you have a bad guest, it's a stress for maybe a week, but if you've got a bad tenant, it's a stress for months. So, it's a good return almost."

The two-day *Property Investors Crash Course* left a lasting impression on them, although at the beginning it forced them out of their comfort zone.

Jake remembers that after arriving they sat at the back of the room. "We were quite nervous and didn't want to get involved. We just wanted to watch and not do anything but then Samuel made us get into teams and find deals. As he often tells students, it's a 'doinar,' not a seminar."

Destiny says the fact they were so young and had never done anything like it before made it difficult. Working with strangers, however, did them 'good' because they learnt how to build relationships.

"We learned a lot by the end and were creeping towards the front."

With six deals safely in the bag, Jake and Destiny are eager to find out more about other ways of making money from real estate. That is why they consider advanced training would be beneficial for them going forward.

Destiny sums up their position: "We want to get more SAs and eventually start buying our own, and look into other avenues as well, like deal sourcing. If we had done the paid training, we would have probably fast forwarded our success, but we've still got here with just the free training."

She wishes they had gone into property earlier, although as Samuel points out to them, they did it early enough. He praises them for being action takers, even when they had people around them questioning what they were doing.

"The first rent-to-rent Destiny and Jake secured is an absolute gem. It just shows that when you go out, knock on doors, call agents and say the right scripts, you will be rewarded. They've gone on to build a nice rent-to-rent portfolio. They're financially free, full time in property and doing incredibly well. To earn the kind of money that they are even in the off season you'd generally have to be something like a barrister who has been to university and studied for six or seven years.

"I've got huge respect for what they've achieved. I know we'll see them on the advanced training later on. Then we can start scaling and doing different things. But the fact they've done this from the crash course is absolutely amazing.

"I really appreciated Destiny's message on Instagram. I get similar messages regularly. That's what gives me the drive and the energy to keep putting out content and running property training even if some of it is free."

DESTINY AND JAKE'S TIPS

"Jake: Don't be scared. Just give it a go. We wouldn't be in the situation we are now if we'd never come to the crash course and tried out serviced accommodation."

"Destiny: What is there to lose coming out of school? You may as well put your all into something rather than going the safe route of I've got to get a full-time job. Give it a crack, especially if you can start with no money."

Chapter 26 – Sam Gallagher

Former hospital porter's life is transformed by property success

Life looked less than rosy in the spring of 2021 for Sam Gallagher. The hospital porter was taking depression tablets after splitting up with his girlfriend. To make matters worse he was in debt, having spent more than £23,000 on property courses which failed to work for him.

Then the 27-year-old came across Samuel Leeds and enrolled on one of his training programmes. As a result, Sam is now financially independent from a portfolio of rent-to-HMOs in Bolton.

His motivation for wanting to go into business is a familiar one. He had a succession of jobs when he was younger, working in warehouses, as well as McDonald's before becoming a porter at Bolton Hospital. It was a role that satisfied him to an extent because he was helping people, especially during the Covid pandemic, he says.

Constantly in his mind, however, was the thought that he wanted to break free from the daily grind of being an employee under the control of others.

"I've always wanted to work for myself. I don't like having a boss and having to answer to a boss. I was always looking for a way out of the nine-to-five life."

Property, Sam realised, presented that opportunity to gain financial freedom and so he went all out to learn how to invest in assets that would make him money. But after spending thousands of pounds on training elsewhere and not pulling off a single deal, Sam was left feeling disillusioned and angry. Despite this, he refused to relinquish his dream of becoming a property entrepreneur.

"That initial training, I would say, wasn't the best but I didn't want to give up. I'm this person who will just keep going and going until I succeed. So, I had to find another way of getting the right training and making it succeed. That's when I discovered Samuel Leeds," he explains.

"I was sceptical because I'd spent all that money and got absolutely nowhere. I said to myself the next decision I make has to be the right decision. I need to be confident that what I do next is going to succeed."

And so, he signed up for Property Investors' *Deal Finding Extravaganza* course which, because of the coronavirus situation, had been put online at that point. It was the perfect solution for Sam because he could do it from home without the need to travel and pay for accommodation.

As soon as he started applying himself to it, he was impressed.

"What I loved about it was there were so many tips and how to's which I picked up from that which weren't in the other training. The beauty of it was that it came along with mentoring as well. It was the important first step to me getting my first deal because it gave me that spark again and that light at the end of the tunnel."

It took Sam about ten months after finishing the DFE to land his first deal. This was not to do with the training, he stresses. As he describes it, 'life got in the way.'

When Sam was just getting started, he had a partner who was concerned about him spending more money on property education. Gradually their relationship crumbled, and they separated.

"In the first couple of months it was a fairy tale. I was on top of the world. I thought it was a perfect relationship. I'm starting to build my business on the way to my first deal but as we all know fairy tales don't last.

"It quickly spiralled out of control," Sam remembers. "I ended up at the doctors on depression tablets. By May I was down and out. But the key thing I would say to everybody, whoever you are, is don't ever give up no matter how bad the situation is."

With the support of the Property Investors community spurring him on, he managed to climb out of the valley back to the mountaintop again.

Sam acknowledges it was his training with Samuel Leeds which enabled him to clinch his first deal – plus being able to get advice from Samuel and his team of coaches. He also had another business mentor who helped him too. Persistence was also an important ingredient in giving him that all-important, long-awaited breakthrough.

He found the deal through an independent agency in Bolton after explaining that he was looking for a landlord who was willing to rent his property to him as a company let. Under the agreement, the owner would receive a guaranteed monthly rent. In exchange, his company would be permitted to rent out the rooms individually at a higher rate and retain the profit.

As a result of this conversation, the agent showed Sam a five-bed HMO which had been occupied for a long time by contractors building a new supermarket in the area. When the job was finished, they had left, leaving the landlord with an empty property suddenly on his hands.

It was that factor which made the landlord more receptive to the idea of a rent-to-rent arrangement, says Sam, because the owner was used to having a long-term, guaranteed rental income. He agreed to pay the landlord £950 a month and to cover the bills. Totting everything up, it amounted to a monthly liability of about £1,500.

Sam admits it was 'scary' signing the contract because he worried that he might have trouble filling the rooms but told himself the system worked.

"One key thing I've heard Samuel say is: walk the a, b, c. Worry about the x, y, z later. So, I just did it."

Nevertheless, it was not a case of walking blindly into such a huge commitment. Sam had done his homework beforehand to make sure it was a viable proposition. He had the advantage too of being able to ask his mentors to check the numbers stacked.

As part of the agreement, Sam had to pay a deposit, in addition to one month's rent which came to a total of £5,000.

"I had no money to finance the deal, but I was taught you don't know who's got money in the bank. Just ask the question. Lo and behold, I asked a friend if he could lend me the money and he said no problem."

Sam agreed to repay it over a year with an interest rate of 10 per cent, using some of the cash to paint and furnish the house.

His investor had been due to get his money back in the summer of 2022 but agreed to extend the loan by another year.

"We'll pay his interest in July but roll the £5,000 over for another 10 per cent," says Sam.

The house has a large attic room which brings in a rent of £500 a month. The monthly charge for a standard room is £400. All bills are included. It leaves him with a profit of just over £600 per month after his expenses. By comparison, at the end of the loan period, he will have paid out £1,000 in interest, plus the £5,000 he borrowed.

Sam secured his second rent-to-rent agreement on a six-bed property which again was already set up as a house share. It needed a 'light refurb' which included painting and furnishing the property and doing some odd jobs to get it ready for renting out.

Once more he borrowed the cash from an investor to do the improvements.

"We quickly got a turnaround on that one. It was a little bit quicker than the first one because we'd learnt lessons from that. So, we got painters to paint the second one, whereas I painted the first one myself. Initially you might need to do it yourself, but you quickly want to get out of that."

The second HMO earns him just over £1,000, giving him an overall profit of £1,600 per month between the two properties under his control.

Sam has also negotiated a third rent-to-rent deal on a property which will be ready for tenants soon. He is expecting to make just over £800 a month on that one. On top of this, he has also had an offer accepted on a five-bedroom house which will net him £1,088 per month.

Sam has experienced no significant issues with any of his properties nor his tenants. He has also been able to fill the rooms quickly. He puts that down to having had the 'right training' and mentoring.

"Our first one was filled in 21 days and the second one in 10 days. In the back of my mind, I thought I need to get this money in quickly. I don't want these rooms to be empty. So, with the first property deal I got, I picked up this tip that while you're trying to get your tenants in as an HMO bang all the rooms on Airbnb and booking.com and rent them out on a nightly basis as serviced accommodation.

"I never thought Bolton would be like this. Every weekend the rooms were full. We were getting bookings during the week. It got to the point where I was getting too many bookings and not enough rooms available. It was crazy."

He chose Bolton as his patch because he lives in the town. It made sense to him to assess his local area first for its potential after completing his training before looking further afield for opportunities.

While being interviewed for Samuel Leeds' popular YouTube *Winners on a Wednesday* show Sam revealed he was about to attend another *Property Investors Crash Course* to get more tips.

"You've got to have the training to be successful. It is important as well to have somebody who's been there and done what you want to do."

He adds: "The hardest part of the journey for me is to not get bogged down with looking ten steps ahead. I literally take it one step at a time. A lot of people look ten steps ahead and it becomes analysis paralysis. They don't move forward."

Sam has a new partner Bethany these days and is on top of the world again after giving up his job in November 2021 to go full-time into property. This time round he refuses to be distracted though. With two failed relationships behind him, he says his property business is his priority now.

"This is where I've become successful. It's made me happy as a person. So, no matter what's around me – any relationships, anything, this has to be number one. When I went into the new relationship, I had to make it clear to her that that's how I am as a person now and she totally understood it. She's always supporting me, telling me how proud she is of me and how much she wants me to do well. Anything I need, she helps with, like cleaning the HMOs. It's so nice."

Samuel is delighted to have played such a key part in Sam's success. He says: "For whatever reason, Sam just didn't gel with the training he'd had previously. Then he came on the *Deal Finding Extravaganza* with me. I remember saying we're going to have to make this guy successful. We were determined. The whole team was encouraging him and he showed a lot of persistence after he recovered from his heartbreak.

"When you're starting out from scratch, and you've got personal issues and debts, you've got to look at the long game. That's what Sam did. He continued investing in himself, even though he was in a really bad situation. He is to be congratulated for doing that."

SAM'S TIPS

"Trust in what you've been taught. Trust that it works and take it one step at a time."

"Make sure you have a business plan and a strategy before you start buying deals."

"When you're looking for a patch, start with where you live. Then branch out to surrounding areas if that area doesn't work."

"Independent agents are a lot more open to creative strategies like rent-to-rent. Go in person and be confident. Say you're looking for a company let, rather than a rent-to-rent arrangement."

Samuel Leeds

Chapter 27 – Prity and Kyle Chauhan

Mother and son team financially free through property in under two years

Two heads are better than one, they say. That is certainly true of Prity and Kyle Chauhan who both love property. The mother and son went into business together after joining Samuel Leeds' academy in November 2020. Less than two years later they are financially independent through implementing the rent-to-rent strategy.

Kyle knew he wanted to make his money from bricks and mortar from the age of just 16. Prity shared his interest. Before her son was born, she used to do up rental properties on a shoestring for a friend.

"She paid me to go shopping, to stage a house. She said I want you to do exactly what you've done in your house. I absolutely loved it and then I was pregnant with Kyle, and I stopped doing all of that," says Prity.

That enthusiasm resurfaced years later when Kyle said he would like to get involved with her in property.

"I've always watched programmes like *Homes under the Hammer* with my mother. We knew we wanted to get into it together, we just didn't know how," explains Kyle.

Prity told her son they needed to get some money first and advised him to take up a trade so that he could at least do some of the work himself if he invested in a property and it needed refurbishing. So, Kyle took up an apprenticeship as a plumber. Meanwhile, she bought a single let by refinancing her home. Then an unforeseen event altered their approach.

Relating the story, Prity says: "I'd gone into hospital for a minor operation. It was supposed to take 30 minutes, but the procedure went horribly wrong. I ended up being taken in for emergency surgery, a four-hour operation."

The former civil servant discovered afterwards that there was a 25 per cent mortality rate for this kind of surgery. Thankfully, she pulled through it, although she was out of action for three months. Recovering at home gave her the chance to look at how she and Kyle could go into business together.

"I got to thinking [about] the children. I'm a single parent. I thought, they're not babies but what if something happened about the financial side of things. Neither of them was working full time. I knew Kyle always wanted to get into property, so I thought let me start to do some research. It was the first time I'd literally had some headspace and time to think about how I could do this."

While searching the internet for information, Prity found Samuel Leeds' YouTube channel. She watched a couple of his *Winners on a Wednesday* interviews featuring successful students and loved what she heard about how the training had helped them achieve their dreams.

In the caption below, there was information about the *Property Investors Crash Course*. The two-day event was free, apart from the £1 registration fee. So, it was a 'no brainer' for them to go along.

Prity and Kyle were accompanied by her partner, and her daughter and boyfriend.

"We were absolutely buzzing. Both nights, after the event, we were like this is the best thing we've ever done."

Afterwards all five of them signed up for the Property Investors Academy. By this point, they had made up their minds to pursue the rent-to-rent strategy. Their training, however, was interrupted when the second national lockdown was imposed to prevent the spread of the coronavirus.

The lockdown prohibited people meeting who were not in their 'support bubble' indoors. Consequently, students who had enrolled on the academy had their memberships paused while all the courses were put online.

Refusing to let that get in their way, Kyle and his mother continued to research their chosen strategy. They had further support from being able to log in to Samuel Leeds' weekly webinar calls. Seeing how others were succeeding gave them the incentive to keep going. Then, when the restrictions were eased, they opted to complete the rent-to-rent module first.

It took about three months for them to pull off their first deal on a seven-bedroom house in Leicester.

"It took a lot of hard work. There were times when we felt down. Are we ever going to do this? Is it right for us? But we persisted with it and eventually got the first one which was great," recalls Kyle.

He was studying full time, while Prity was still employed, managing services in the buildings where civil servants work.

"It was really difficult. We started after five every day. We'd switch the laptops on and go through the training ourselves because it was online in the lockdown," she says.

They studied every night for up to two hours. Then Kyle started calling agents.

"I remember before doing any of the training I didn't really have a lot of confidence at all. I didn't think it was right for me at first. It was the same when I began the plumbing training. I thought, is this for me or not?

"I remember attempting to ring agents. It lasted around 10 seconds before I'd put the phone down. I just thought, is this really for me? But in the end, I stayed consistent with it and here we are now."

He adds: "Going to the *Property Investors Crash Course* and being around like-minded people really helped build my confidence up and attending an event called *Tell the World*."

This course teaches students to tell as many people as possible, including family and friends, that they are property investors with the aim of attracting potential deals and customers.

Like all businesses, there are ups and down and challenges to overcome. Kyle and Prity experienced this at the beginning of their journey. Overjoyed at having got their first deal, they rolled up their sleeves to prepare it for the market, only to see it turn into a disaster due to a catalogue of errors.

The pair had negotiated a rent-free period to give them time to renovate the rundown house before bringing in tenants. However, instead of letting the rooms individually, as they became ready, they waited until they were all done up.

"That was the first mistake, we realised afterwards, because we carried on past the rent-free period still doing the other rooms up. It meant we ended up paying another month's rent without anyone in the house," she says.

They made other blunders, admits Kyle. "There was a lot of work involved. We identified we should have got other tradesmen in like painters, for example. We ended up running past the six-week grace period just solely from painting and decorating."

What they did do right was to use their network to get themselves out of a hole, as Samuel had taught them in their training. So, they enlisted their family and friends to help them finish the job.

Prity says after all the hard work was done, the three-storey house looked beautiful, and they were ready to fill the rooms. But then they adopted the wrong tactics by showing prospective tenants all the rooms and insisting they bring documentation with them.

"I remembered from Samuel's training you should always secure it [the tenancy] at the point they come to view the property."

Prity asked potential customers before they came to view the property to bring a deposit, a holding fee and proof of identification with them. She told them they would then carry out some checks.

"For some reason they all said, 'Well, at the moment, can I just think about it? I want to just go. We didn't know what to do. So, they'd just go [to see the house]."

During a Monday Mastermind call with their mentor and other Property Investors Academy members, Prity asked for help.

"We absolutely love that because when we're feeling really low and wondering whether we're going to do this we get on the call. Everyone is winning or sharing problems and helping each other out. So, I just piped up Samuel, 'I'm having a real problem and I'm not sleeping.

"We'd already paid one month's rent out of our own pockets, and it wasn't tenanted. I thought the rent is £2,200 a month. I can't keep doing this. I just shouted up on the Mastermind call and Samuel asked me how he could help. I really appreciated that.

"I said I'd love it if you would come and just tell me what I'm doing wrong.

It was great because not only did he come but people on the network were all offering me advice. Like Samuel always says, your network is your net worth and it's so true. And the more we're learning and getting support, the more we're being motivated. It's amazing."

When the Property Investors chairman visited Kyle and Prity at the property, they found a tenant straight away. Together, they produced a video about how to fill rooms quickly. They organised block viewings, refreshed their advertisement and showed people one room at a time.

A year later the house is making them a profit of £1,200 a month.

Kyle says: "Since Samuel came round and helped us it's been easier to get tenants in. We use different platforms like SpareRoom, Facebook Marketplace, Gumtree and OpenRent. We still make sure the advert is live in case we have other opportunities, and I can show them our other rent-to-rents. I would recommend that for anyone."

Prity and her son have gone on to clinch two more rent-to-rent agreements, with more in the offing. One of the things which has helped them is changing their mindset. On the *Financial Freedom Intensive,* students are taught to raise their financial thermostat – to avoid the danger of just stopping when they start earning what they used to in their job.

Kyle and Prity also make a point of visiting estate agents. Whereas previously Prity thought agents were their enemy, she now tries to build a rapport with them. All of a sudden they are receiving calls from agents, offering them more properties.

"They've got to know, like and trust you. It's easier for them to do that if they can see you face to face. They're more inclined to say yes to your face than over the phone," points out Kyle.

He oversees their second rent-to-rent house which is two minutes away from the first one. It has six bedrooms and two bathrooms and is generating a monthly profit of £1,000. His mother looks after the other house under their control.

Kyle intends to go into property full time when he finishes his plumbing apprenticeship, having already established a network of tradesmen, including friends who are builders.

"What works well with me, and my mum, is that I'm the hands on side of it and she's got the business side of it."

Kyle also used his contacts to obtain a buy, refurbish, refinance project through an estate agent he had worked for every fortnight when he was still at school. He used to answer the telephone and got to know the workings of the property market.

The agent, who lives on the same street as him and has been a family friend for 15 years, passed on the deal to him.

"Samuel says tell everyone what you're doing. That's exactly what I did. The agent gave me this. It's a probate property off market. I've managed to get it £45,000 below market value."

Prity and her partner are part-funding the purchase of the house for £480,000. She persuaded two investors to help finance the acquisition after pitching the deal on Property Elevators, a Dragon's Den style TV show.

A Property Investors coach assisted her in preparing her script which she delivered to five investors who complimented her on her presentation.

The refurbishment is costing £130,000 and they are setting aside another £20,000 for legal fees, bringing the total spend to £630,000. They originally planned to turn it into an HMO, but the property was in an Article 4 area which limits such developments. So, they are converting it into self-contained flats on the advice of one of their mentors.

Prity says they had not thought of doing this before, but it will make the seven-bedroom house worth more. The end value is expected to be around

£840,000, which will allow them to pull out all their money.

She says she is proud of her 23-year-old son and the fact he is now set up for life.

"That is the path I wanted him to take. My daughter is doing something similar. That's exactly what I wanted for my children to be entrepreneurs, to not have a nine to five and be in the rat race."

Samuel is impressed by their progress so far.

"I always say on the academy there are only two reasons why you can fail – one because you don't take any action and when you get stuck you don't ask for help. Prity and Kyle did ask for help on the Mastermind.

"They have done everything step by step from the training and it's worked beautifully. They came to the academy and learned but they've also crewed at events and helped so many people. I've really appreciated them."

PRITY AND KYLE'S TIPS

"Give value first. Serve first and success follows."

"If you want people to invest in you, you've got to first invest in yourself."

"Stay consistent and persistent."

Chapter 28 – Lewis Dawson and Mel Cox

Two academy students make £14K in a week from deal sourcing!

Ask Mel Coxon what she does for a living, she will tell you she and her business partner Lewis Dawson find lucrative property deals and sell them to investors. In just one week they earned £14,500 from deal sourcing and yet Mel had not even heard of it when she saw the New Year in, in 2022. In fact, she had no experience of property, other than saving up for a deposit for her first house.

It was Lewis who got started in property during the pandemic and then Mel, an ex-employee of his, joined him. They became members of Samuel Leeds' academy and now benefit from using other strategies as well.

Lewis ran a marketing company for six years but always had a passion for property. When Covid hit, he began looking into investing in real estate.

He purchased his first buy-to-let – a small flat in Newcastle-upon-Tyne where he is based – then decided he wanted something bigger and bought a detached house which he moved into. When he became bored with living there after three months, he rented it out.

After this, he acquired the estate of a deceased person with the intention of renovating it, using his many connections with local builders.

It was at this point that Lewis became aware of Samuel Leeds and the different methods which could be used to derive the maximum profit from his investment. One option, he had not previously considered was renting rooms out individually, as opposed to having a single tenant.

Lewis was sent a link to Amelia Asante's interview with Samuel which was filmed for his popular *Winners on a Wednesday* YouTube series featuring successful students. He sent it to Mel, urging her to watch it and then enrolled on a *Property Investors Crash Course* in Leeds in December 2021.

After attending the crash course, he made up his mind to go into property full time, giving Mel the choice to either stay in her job or come on board with him.

Mel, who was working as his head of operations, was in no doubt about what she wanted to do.

"I said, 'Let's take the risk and go into property. I quit my job and now I'm his business partner."

In the spring of 2022, she went into property full time too, from having had no knowledge or experience of it before.

Lewis and Mel swung into action to get their business up and running.

The academy gave them the knowledge they needed to become professional deal sourcers – and they wasted no time in picking up business. They earned a £14,500 from commissions in one week after selling four deals together, says Lewis.

They are also dipping into other strategies now to expand their activities.

They clinched a rent-to-rent agreement and hope to buy a piece of land next to a caravan park. If planning consent is granted, they will either build on the site to provide serviced accommodation or sell off the plot.

Potentially there is 'big money' in it but as with any development it is 'slow money,' because it takes time to go through the process.

Fortunately, Lewis has the rental income from his houses which amounts to around £3,000 a month, plus they have both earned money from deal selling.

Lewis joined the academy just after completing the *Property Investors Deal Selling Masterclass,* with Mel signing up soon afterwards.

They say becoming educated in property has accelerated their progress.

Lewis describes the network on the academy as incredible.

"I had a few coaches who were very successful in my previous industry. I realised by coming to Samuel's crash course and the first deal sourcing event that if you get in with the guys and girls who are doing what you want to do, you're going to be able to progress way faster.

"Then, when we came back from the deal selling event, I booked us on as many networking events as possible. We met people in Birmingham, Newcastle and all across the north-east. That's what made the biggest difference.

"Once people started seeing us doing well on our social media it gave a lot of people belief and it all just came from the network and the academy."

His buy, refurbish, refinance scheme came about through the connections he established with auction teams in the north-east. Two of these links were with men who used to work for his company. When they realised their former boss was in property, they began offering him lots of deals.

One was for a house which failed to sell when it went under the hammer. Lewis was given the opportunity to buy it. However, he only had one day to reach an agreement as it was being auctioned off again the following day.

He managed to secure the property for £71,000, spending only £5,000 on the refurbishment on top of that as he did a lot of the work himself.

His training again gave him the expertise and skills to turn it into a four-bed HMO.

"I rented it out to three of my ex-employees which was handy and then we refinanced on it. It cost me about £30,000 all in with the deposit and refurb. I managed to pull out £33,000 from that deal and now it's generating £1,400 a month."

The valuation on the house, which is ten minutes away from the centre of Newcastle, came in at £115,000 once it had been improved. Not only that, the money he pulled out was tax-free.

Their social media manager publicised the deal on TikTok. To their utter astonishment, the post attracted one million views.

Lewis and Mel agree with their mentor that it is essential to have people around you who are backing you all the way and are like-minded.

"Environment is everything," says Lewis. "That's what I love about the courses as well because they come round so regularly. If you feel you're hitting a bit of a lull you go to a course and you're straight back up again.

"And you build that relationship up with people on the academy. It's like going back and seeing friends again."

Mel and Lewis send out their deals to a list of investors who they found through their contacts on the Property Investors Academy and taking part in networking events.

"To start with you don't have any investors and you have a couple of deals come through. Then you have loads of investors and no deals. Now we get thrown deals all the time but haven't got enough investors for the deals. So, we can always do with more investors," stresses Lewis.

Mel, who is based in Sunderland, says they have a good relationship with estate agents and obtain a lot of off market deals. They also go out looking for opportunities.

"You start noticing more things when you're driving – can I get a lease option on this or can I do this."

Lewis describes her as the superstar when it comes to organising their operation.

"I'm on the ground, going to the viewings and spending time with the builders. Mel puts everything in place and tells me where I can and can't go."

He frequently views properties for fellow academy members who live too far away to do it themselves. Other investors have neither the time nor the know-how to find a deal. A key part of the service Lewis and Mel offer includes negotiating a good price on a property.

Being a deal sourcer is not without its problems, although sometimes they are nice ones. One morning they woke up to the realisation that they had sold three deals in a day which caused them an administrative headache. Teamwork pulled them through, says Mel.

"We were like how do we handle this? I was typing up all the contracts and sending them out to each investor. Lewis was talking to the estate agent. It is very stressful, but the rewards afterwards outweigh this."

Lewis says they were under pressure to quickly get everything in order as the investors had already paid them their fees. They were also eager to maintain a good customer service experience to encourage the investors to use their services again.

Mel and Lewis also discovered that clients can be reluctant to part with their money. So now they require a finder's fee before giving out all the information about a deal. Mel says they have trained their investors to know that unless they pay upfront, the deal will be offered to the next customer who expresses an interest and puts their money on the table.

One customer lost out on a deal because he failed to pay the fee straight away. He soon came back to them for another deal which they had emailed out to their list. All their investors are offered a 14-day cooling off period to consider whether they still want to proceed.

Mel and Lewis learnt on the academy that they need to get paid before the completion of a property sale to reflect the hard work they have put in. This not only includes identifying a potential money-spinner, but also researching the area, carrying out the negotiations, calculating the return on investment and presenting the figures to the investor – in short packaging and distributing the deal.

"We've made the mistakes. We trusted investors when we maybe shouldn't have done and we've learnt that lesson," admits Lewis.

They both praise the quality of their training, believing it to be fundamental to their success. Lewis says he loved the *Deal Selling Masterclass*.

"It gets you on the phone. We're quite comfortable with that anyway because Mel's always been on the phone, and I've always been face-to-face with customers. But it is so streamlined. You go from having a lead to being taught how you package that and get it ready for an investor. It's amazing."

Mel's target was to earn as much as she used to in her old job within six months.

"We've just made half my yearly salary in a week. I couldn't believe it when it was actually in the account. I've never seen that much money!

"It's who you know and what you know but without the academy and the network we would have never been able to get where we are today."

They are now setting their sights on tying up some rent-to-serviced accommodation deals in Europe. They were due to fly out to Portugal to view properties when Samuel gave them their moment in the spotlight by interviewing them for *Winners on a Wednesday*.

It is this ambition which drives them on to achieve even more. Lewis also wants to be able to help his family, including his father who worked as a bricklayer until he was 70.

"That's where I get the passion from. Also, I want to be on a beach somewhere making money while I'm sleeping. We've set a goal that for every £10,000 we make we go on holiday. The goal is to be on holiday every week!"

Samuel says he has enjoyed working with them and seeing how they are developing.

"It's good to also work with people who are already having a bit of success in property, like Lewis was. They're already going to do well on their own, but what we can do is help them grow faster and bigger and have fun doing it. Both Lewis and Mel have worked extremely hard and deserve their success."

He added: "I once sold six deals in one afternoon. There is an aftermath because the investor wants to be hand-held and have someone to do the due diligence and listen to them. It can be quite stressful but at the same time the best deals you find you keep yourself. So, it's just the perfect business to do in property."

*Since being interviewed for *Winners on a Wednesday* Lewis and Mel have begun working independently. They continue to thrive in their property businesses.

LEWIS AND MEL'S TIPS

Mel: "Get educated and network. Samuel's energy is amazing. When you come to an event you feel super re-charged. You've got that constant support and the mentoring calls. It's great having that network there."

Lewis: "Your network is your net worth. Samuel has got so much on and yet he's still on the calls every Monday night. That's massive, as is the team he has created."

Chapter 29 – Reza Askari

From surviving on £1 frozen meals to making a hot £10K a month

Property excites Reza Askari and why not? The Iranian-born entrepreneur lives in one of the greatest cities in the world, London, earning around £10,000 a month on average from a large HMO rent-to-rent portfolio. He eats fine food, buys whatever takes his fancy and dictates his work patterns. In short, Reza is the epitome of a smart, self-made man.

His story is one of believing in himself and taking risks. He is also living proof that you can launch a business even if you have no money. In 2019, he was unemployed and living in Birmingham with his family. Then he one day he made a momentous decision.

"I moved to London in 30 minutes. One day I came home. I woke up my mum who was downstairs in our house in Birmingham. I just had my bag. She said, 'What are you doing?' I said you know what I'm tired of living in Birmingham. I just want to go to London.

"She said, 'What are you going to do?' I said, 'I don't know, but I'm just going, and I'll find a flat.'"

His friends and relatives told him he was stupid to go to such an expensive place without a plan, but Reza was insistent. True to his word, he travelled to the capital where he found somewhere to stay and got a job in a bar.

That was the start of his journey. From there he found employment with a letting agency before setting up his own company. Now he controls 19 properties owned by one landlord, including apartments and HMOs.

Samuel Leeds played a key role in setting him on the path to self-employment. He met the Property Investors chairman on one of his *Financial Freedom Challenges* and later signed up for his training.

Reza was the letting agent who gave Samuel and his student, Amelia Asante, a tour of a penthouse apartment in Canary Wharf during the challenge. He recognised Samuel immediately because he had been watching his property videos online.

"I was shocked. I thought what's Samuel Leeds doing here," recalls Reza.

It was while he was still working in a bar and sharing a room with seven others in Whitechapel in London's East End that he first came across Samuel.

"I've always been excited about property. It's something I love. I was trying to find a way to get into the market, but many people told me you can't do it. So, I started to explore YouTube and Google to find out how to get into property. When I typed property in YouTube the first video that came up was by Samuel Leeds."

Reza began listening to his large selection of videos and was inspired by the message that anyone can make a living in the property industry with the right training, hard work and initiative.

Determined to have a go at it, Reza walked into a serviced accommodation agency and asked for help.

"I said I don't know anything. I want to start. Would you help me?'

His direct approach worked. The agency took him on on a fortnight's trial, telling him he would be hired if they liked him. Reza handed in his resignation at the bar straightaway, taking a risk that by the time his two-week notice period was up he would be offered a permanent position.

Reza stayed there for less than year in the end before moving to a letting agency and then meeting his guru, Samuel, in person.

"That's when my inspiration level went much higher. I thought, let's try something else because Samuel Leeds is telling me you don't need money to start a business."

Reza began by calling his contacts and asking if they would let him manage their properties under a rent-to-rent arrangement. He would pay them a fixed rent each month and then rent out the accommodation at a higher rate, retaining the profit.

"I said it is corona. I don't have money, but I know how to do it. Would you be happy to give your properties to me, no deposit, no first month's rent?

The first two owners he rang laughed at him but the third one gave him a chance. He offered him two houses on condition that he filled them fully with tenants within a month. It was make or break, but Reza rose to the challenge. In four days, all seven rooms in both houses were rented out, he says.

"I paid the landlord – he was quite happy with the methods I'd gone through – and slowly he gave me more and more properties."

All of Reza's rent-to-rent properties are in Canary Wharf, London's plush business district which is also home to some of the richest people in the world.

His average monthly profit is just under £10,000, although some months it is lower.

"HMOs have costs. Sometimes you need furniture and this and that. However, the lowest I make these days is £6,000 to £7,000. It's guaranteed 100 per cent. It's fantastic. Two years ago, I was making £1,200 a month in a bar but now I work two days a week or less than that."

Reza says Samuel's videos and classes literally 'changed his life.'

"I've done my own research as well, but it all started with Samuel showing and telling people that it's actually not that hard. You just need to be focused and do it."

Working in a letting agency before setting himself up in business gave him an advantage, Reza admits.

"When you work with a landlord or an investor it gives them that assurance that you can take care of the property and you know what you are doing. But then again if you have no experience of letting you can still do it. You have to study and do some courses."

Although his previous work gave him a helping hand, he was hampered in other ways. Reza built up his rent-to-rent portfolio while on a five-year work visa in Britain. Due to his status, he could not apply for a loan to start his business. It meant he had an overdraft of £200 on the day he registered his company.

As his visa is about to expire, he cannot obtain a mortgage either to buy a house. However, he is hoping to renew his visa soon so that he can get onto the property ladder himself.

Reza lacked finance, but his determination to succeed kept him going and he soon saw the money rolling in.

After tenanting his first two houses, he was left with nearly £1,000 once he had paid the landlord his rent, he says. The young entrepreneur was astonished that in four days he had made almost what he was earning per month as a barman.

Reza capitalised on his success by enrolling on Property Investors' *Deal Selling Masterclass*. Within a fortnight he had sold one deal, picking up a commission of £2,000. Just that one deal covered the cost of the £1,995 course. He then sold another deal in a day.

"It was exactly what I used to do, but Samuel showed me that I could charge people for finding the deal."

As with any endeavour in life, there is risk, he says. Once two of his tenants failed to pay the rent. Making sure the landlord received his guaranteed rent was essential to him, so he made up the shortfall himself.

The alternative to not taking risks is to remain in a poorly paid job, Reza believes. One way he has lowered the odds of a tenant defaulting on their rent is to only accept professional people. In his experience, they always pay up.

He also avoids mixing students with professionals and people on benefits because they come in and out at different times of the day, disturbing each other.

"It doesn't work at all. Someone wakes up at about 4am. Someone comes back at 2am. They bother each other. The tenants are unhappy. After a couple of months, they leave you, so you lose your business."

He took over a portfolio of eight properties in the spring of 2022 from a company which, in his opinion, made the mistake of mixing tenants.

Reza also firmly believes in having a good contract in place to minimise any potential for loss. This was something which his mentor Samuel recommended. One method, which he has adopted of protecting himself from rising energy costs, is to introduce a fair use policy.

All the bills are included in the rent, but if they exceed an agreed credit limit the tenants share the additional cost.

"For example, I just rented a room this morning (April 2022) and the bill for that three-bedroom house comes to nearly £130 a month. I've told the tenants this house has a £150 credit limit for all bills included in the contract. If it's less than that no problem, but if your bills go to £200 the three rooms should pay £15 each."

He implemented the rule after discovering some of his tenants were at home for just two hours a day but were leaving the heating on all the time. It left him having to fork out nearly £300 when he was expecting to only pay half that amount.

The bill in fact comes to £130 a month but he has set the credit limit at £150 so that even if his tenants waste some energy they are not penalised.

"They didn't care because all the bills were included. Now [with the new contract] they turn the heating off. It's good because since I changed my contract all my energy bills have come down from what I even expected."

Reza's landlord has a total of 50 properties which he hopes in time will all be passed over to him to rent out. There are clear benefits for them both, says Reza, in having a rent-to-rent agreement for the 19 properties he has taken on so far.

"He could hire someone else to do it, but he is a super busy person. He doesn't care if I make £10,000 or £100,000 on these properties. What he cares about is getting his rent. Each property is taken care of, and he does not pay any management fee.

"I make £10,000 a month but he saves £10,000 a month on not paying the commissions and he's got a rent guaranteed for the next five to ten years."

Reza employs a team of trusted handymen and plumbers who are on call to deal with any repairs which need to be done. Tenants call them directly if they have a problem and Reza gets sent the bill, freeing up his time. Any handyman who overcharges him is replaced.

The pandemic was raging when Reza set up his HMO business, but that did not deter him.

"I thought the time that no one opens a business I will open a business. If I can't rent out a couple of properties in one of the biggest and best cities in the world, it's ridiculous. I have to do it or lose the opportunity."

His properties range in size from a one-bed flat with two rooms to six-bedroom houses.

When he started out, he was up at 5am so that he could do some research and training before going off to work.

"I set a plan for myself and followed it for three months. In that time my life changed."

It was that same single-minded mentality which drove him to leave the security of his home, despite his family and friends warning him not to go.

"Many people said, oh you can't do it, but I knew from the beginning I can do it, I want to do it and I will do it. I told them, 'Guys, I'm leaving. When I call you back I'm someone else.' I called some of them back and I was someone else. I was a guy who all of them thought I couldn't be, but I made it in less than three years. If you believe in yourself, you'll do it."

The training has been crucial in transforming his fortunes.

"The energy you get from it motivates you. I also like the fact that Samuel shows you what to do and then forces you to do it. You can't run away. You have to do it."

These days Reza describes himself as a big spender.

"When I lived in Whitechapel I couldn't afford to eat that much. I would have to go to Iceland and buy a £1 frozen Bolognese.

"Now I go to the best restaurants in the city. I buy whatever I want. I go wherever I want, and I set my own times. If I'm not in the mood to work today I just don't work. If I want to work more, I'll do it."

Samuel says: "I'm inspired by Reza's story. He may have had no money, but what he did have was courage and experience. It's incredible what he's achieved with nothing in one of the most expensive parts of the UK. He's found his niche and now he's about to launch his own letting agency. I'm excited to be helping him reach a whole new level."

REZA'S TIPS

"Don't start a business and then think you can learn later. If you lose someone's trust once you've lost it forever. Educate yourself before doing anything."

"Attend networking events. You could know how to do it and have the money but if you don't have the connections, you don't have anything."

"Check your area. Find out what price you can rent out a property for and what type of person you are targeting as a tenant."

"I do a lot of research on the market to see how people have failed and then don't do that."

"I look for investors – people who own lots of properties. I call my landlord once a week. That way I save time instead of renting multiple properties from different landlords."

Chapter 30 – Jordan Williams-Weekes and Jahmeil Davis

Cousins inspired by Samuel Leeds' videos making £4K a month from property they don't own

Cousins Jordon Williams-Weekes and Jahmeil Davis dreamed of making money from property from an early age after being inspired by TV programmes such as *Homes Under the Hammer*. Like a lot of people, however, they thought they needed cash to do that. So, towards the end of 2020, they started saving hard to buy an investment property.

It was only when Jordon discovered Samuel Leeds that they realised there was another way of getting a foothold in the industry, other than the traditional route they had planned to go down.

The strategy which got them started was rent-to-rent and already, after just over a year in property, their income is double what they expected it to be. Thanks to their training with Property Investors, which taught them how to negotiate and raise finance, they now manage an HMO and three serviced accommodation properties in Coventry and Leicester.

All four were no-money-down deals which made them a clean profit of £3,800 in April (2022). Jordon and Jahmeil also learnt how to systemise their business. This gives them plenty of time to look for more deals as they only spend 10 to 15 hours a week managing their properties.

Their journey to becoming property entrepreneurs began when Jordon contacted his cousin one day to tell him about some content on the internet which he thought would be of interest to Jahmeil.

"Jordon said: 'Have you seen this guy on YouTube, Samuel Leeds? Watch one of his videos and tell me what you think," recalls Jahmeil.

"So, I started watching them and then messaged Jordon saying this guy's a genius. We have to try to do something about this. What Samuel was saying was resonating with me. It was like he was speaking to us."

Jordon was equally excited at the possibilities opening up to them of getting into property.

"When we saw that potentially we might get into it in another way than the conventional one we were all over it, just binge watching the videos.

"The way we were looking at it was we'll both get into a job and save up as much as possible to get an auction property or something like that. Samuel showed us how much of a stupid idea that was."

After soaking up all the information they could from the YouTube vidoes, they attended a free *Property Investors Crash Course* and then signed up for advanced, paid-for training. Jordon had only recently made redundant, and so it was a test of his commitment. However, he knew that they had to make it work, having been hugely impressed by Samuel as a trainer. His decisiveness paid off.

They took the *Rent-to-Rent Accelerator* course online which enabled them to clinch their first deal but not before losing out on another potential money-spinning opportunity.

"When we went to one viewing, we thought it was just an HMO. Looking back, it was in Coventry centre by the train station. It would have worked perfectly as an SA but at that point in our journey we hadn't been educated enough to know we didn't have to use it as an HMO. We could have used it as a serviced accommodation," says Jahmeil.

Persistence proved to be the vital factor that got Jordon and Jahmeil, who are based in Dudley, just outside Birmingham, their initial breakthrough. They sent out 200 letters to landlords, setting out in bullet points the benefits of doing business with them.

"We said we could provide a hassle-free approach and a guaranteed monthly rent which would give the landlord free time," Jahmeil explains.

Jordon adds: "We also put in the fact that we were just coming out of Covid. We tried to use that as an advantage because I think landlords were panicking that they might not be able to get tenants. It allowed us to say we can still find you tenants."

Out of around ten responses, they obtained a viewing of an eight-bed HMO. In their discussions with the landlady, they established that she lacked the time to manage the house share herself. At that point they went away to work out how much they could afford to pay her and still make a profit.

Their offer of £2,037 per month was specific deliberately – a tip they had picked up from their mentor Samuel to suggest that this was their maximum bid and there was no room for negotiation.

"We factored in £2,050 and thought we may as well knock £13 off. It looked a bit more solid," says Jordon.

Reassured by their confident pitch, the landlady accepted their offer, aware too that it was a risk-free proposition for her as they would be responsible for finding tenants. As they had contacted her directly, they were not required to supply references nor pay a deposit.

The rent-to-rent arrangement was sealed in April 2021, and Jahmeil and Jordon agreed to take on the property a few months later. This gave Jahmeil and Jordon time to rent out the rooms.

They asked the landlady if they could have the keys once a week to get some tenants in. They also negotiated a two-week rent-free period. This meant that from April to September, when the contract officially started, they could fill the rooms before they had to pay the landlady her rent.

The only hurdle left was finding £3,000 for furniture. This was a problem because all their money had gone on education and setting up their company.

Luckily, one of the courses they had attended was about joint ventures and raising finance. So, they managed to find an investor to lend them the cash at a fixed interest rate of ten per cent.

By the end of September that year, the house was fully occupied. They rent it out for £3,600 a month. After deducting £600 for utility bills and the rent to the landlady, their profit is around £900, says Jameil.

They struggled to find their second deal and so invested in more education with Property Investors about managing HMOs and serviced accommodation. As a result, they secured a rent-to-rent agreement on an apartment. Again, it came about through approaching the landlord directly, this time through the OpenRent website.

"The best thing we found out with OpenRent is that because it's direct, the rapport can be built straight away," Jahmeil points out.

"We viewed the apartment on Christmas Eve. The landlord loved what we were looking to do with the property which was to rent it out as serviced accommodation.

"As we finished the viewing, because the rapport was already built up, he said to us, 'I've got another one in this building. It hasn't been listed yet. Do you want to have a look at it?'

"It was on the same level as the one we'd just seen, if not better. We made him an offer for this the following day, and he accepted our offer for the other apartment as well. So, we went to find one and ended up getting two."

The importance of picking up the telephone and booking viewings was drummed into them on their training with Property Investors. As Jordon and Jahmeil had experienced themselves, just one viewing can generate more leads and deals.

During one session Jordon teamed up with another student to ring agents and book property viewings. It taught him a valuable lesson which was to not overthink a situation.

"Effectively I was factoring in too much due diligence. Before I'd even made the call, I was thinking will the figures work? How much can I pay? Whereas if I just picked up the phone and made the call to get the viewing, I could figure out the rest later. That was a big tip.

"We got five viewings. We were up on stage. Everyone was cheering for us."

The cousins have systemised their serviced accommodation business by installing key safes so that guests can let themselves in. They also have a 'brilliant' power team, particularly in Coventry, says Jahmeil. When one tenant complained about the toilet being blocked, they called their plumber who fixed it the next day.

Jordon admits that at first they found it overwhelming going from managing an HMO to then taking on three SA's in quick succession, especially as they did not have the right power team in place.

As newcomers to the business of property, they were also operating on a shoestring budget with rents due every month to their landlords.

Despite that they remained optimistic, having been schooled by their trainers to expect tough times on the road to success.

"We just said we're way too far in. We've got things we want to accomplish in life. We're already in the middle of the ocean. To stop would be as bad as going forward," says Jordon.

Jahmeil says: "It's easy to look back and think of the mistakes we made but how far we've come since the point we started has been great. Why can't we keep going forward?"

Being part of a supportive friendship group of young entrepreneurs helps. Although they work in different sectors, they can still share ideas about scaling up and marketing, and observe how they each operate.

Their family is also backing them all the way. Jordon tells a story about how their mothers, who are sisters, berated them one night as they set off to watch a football match.

"They said to us, 'You can't be going out. You're getting complacent. You need to focus all the time.' They're more onto us than we are!"

Jordon and Jahmeil believe the most important thing they have learnt is to be action-takers. On a day off, they went to Leicester to speak to letting agents. Jahmeil had been hesitant about going, but then changed his mind.

"We hadn't been out of our comfort zone. So, I said let's do it. We drove to Leicester and went to six letting agents. That's where the Leicester SA came from."

They credit Samuel Leeds and his team of coaches for giving them the knowledge to succeed and the confidence to keep going.

"At some point you pick up the phone to call an agent and something changes. It just clicks. That's down to the education. Once you get educated and you know what you've got to say it's hard not to prosper in the end."

Jordon says the online training gave them the 'technical fundamentals' to get a deal, but when they went to a physical event they were bowled over by the atmosphere and being able to bounce ideas off people.

"I remember on the first day it went on till about nine at night after a 10am start. If that was a normal job or even another education course, you'd be tired and ready to KO. But at that course the energy and just being around like-minded people was amazing."

His business partner agrees: "The energy in the room is brilliant. You get immersed in it and then you get carried away."

Jahmeil and Jordon are keen to celebrate their achievements but then to move on as they feel they are nowhere near where they want to be yet. They are also motivated by a desire to help others.

Jordon says: "I've seen where my mum and my sister have come from and what they've done to make ends meet. So, it's engrained in me to be able to elevate my family.

"We also want to help other people and one day be in a position of giving, not just receiving."

Samuel is full of praise for his two students: "Some people say, 'I can't do rent-to-rents because I can't pass the referencing.' In Jordon and Jahmeil's case they didn't need to get references for their first deal because the landlady trusted them and warmed to them as people.

"Another objection I hear is, 'I ain't got the money.' On this occasion Jahmeil and Jordon didn't need any money. It was a perfect deal. Now they have a rent-to-rent portfolio and are financially independent. They deserve everything they've achieved."

JORDON'S TIPS

"You need to be an action taker. If you're just a thinker, you won't get anything   done."

"Have a real strong reason why you're doing this and what you want to achieve. That will keep you going."

"We're super conservative with our figures. We'd rather get a lot more than we were expecting than less."

JAHMEIL'S TIPS

"Forget what anybody else says. Follow your own mind and make sure you just do it."

"Make sure you believe in yourself regardless of anything and you can get through any situation. Just keep being persistent."

Final Thoughts

I hope you have enjoyed reading about the remarkable progress of the students featured in this book and have been inspired by their property journeys.

They had four vital things in common. They all...

1. **TOOK MASSIVE ACTION:** To be successful you have to take big steps while others just talk about it. Implementation and hard work are key to being an entrepreneur.

2. **HAD BELIEF:** You need to believe in yourself and in the process. You will manifest what you expect to happen. Show a little faith and don't listen to the doubters.

3. **GOT CREATIVE:** Problems are easy to find, but winners find solutions not problems. When it seems everything is going wrong, you need to get super creative and never take 'no' for an answer.

4. **GAINED KNOWLEDGE:** Property is the second best investment you can make - the best is yourself. All of these people decided to get trained and attended my property investment training programmes. Once you have the knowledge nobody can ever take it from you.

If you embrace these four attributes, don't be surprised when you start getting crazy results and maybe one day you will feature in one of these volumes.

If you have enjoyed these short stories and want to learn how you can achieve similar success, you can get a free ticket to my Property Investors Crash Course. For more information visit: www.property-investors.co.uk

Have you already become financially free from my strategies and teachings? I would love to hear from you on social media. Alternatively, simply email team@property-investors.co.uk

Warmest wishes,

Samuel Leeds

Printed in Great Britain
by Amazon

19681903R00149